FOR THE LOVE OF CANCER

A PASSIONATE PURSUIT TO UNDERSTAND LIFE, DEATH, AND SPIRITUALITY

BY

JULIE DAVIS TITTENHOFER

For The Love of Cancer
A Passionate Pursuit to Understand Life, Death, and Spirituality
Copyright © 2018 by Julie Davis-Tittenhofer
Cover designed by Nehmen-Kodner: www.n-kcreative.com

Library of Congress Control Number: 2018949940
ISBN-13:   Paperback: 978-1-64398-038-6

Printed in the United States of America

LitFire LLC
1-800-511-9787
www.litfirepublishing.com
order@litfirepublishing.com

DEDICATION

This book is dedicated in loving memory of my husband, Robert Nick Tittenhofer, Jr., and is also dedicated to you, the reader, for having the courage to face the many life trials you have been given. It is my belief that you are not reading this book by accident, but rather, as part of a much larger, predestined plan.

I am eternally grateful to my mother who encouraged me to take a leap of faith and write this book. Without her love and support, this book would not exist. I would also like to thank my former pastor and friend, Dave Willis, and other close friends for giving me the inspiration and content found within the pages.

ABOUT THE AUTHOR

Julie Davis-Tittenhofer is a former lawyer, healthcare administration consultant, and seriel entrepreneur. She is also the founder of *Inspirit-Widowed Young Support Group, Inc.* Having been her husband's caregiver through a long battle with colon cancer and then losing him in a tragic accident, she has journeyed through life, love, death, grief and spirituality.

A member of the Georgia Bar Association and the American Bar Association, Julie graduated from Mercer University School of Law and went on to practice civil litigation before returning to work in healthcare. Most recently, Julie found a way to combine her love for healthcare with her entrepreneurial spirit and founded Pura Vida Body & Mind Spa, Inc. Despite her busy schedule, Julie continues to give of her time when young widows and widowers call, helping them heal from their grief while simultaneously uncovering their life purpose.

CONTENTS

ACKNOWLEDGMENTS

I have enormous gratitude to Pastor Dave Willis, who unknowingly gave me the tools to write my testimony in this book. Had I not met him, I would not be who I am today, and this book certainly would not exist. Dave taught me many things along the way, beginning with our first meeting. I will never forget the words he said— "I don't believe in accidents"—meaning our coming together was planned by God for some perfect reason and at the perfect time. I later learned the full meaning of that very simple statement.

To my mother and my friend, I cannot thank you enough for your unending support, even when at times finding comforting words was difficult. You have shared much of my heartache during my life trials, and you have celebrated my successes. For this, I am eternally grateful. You are the matriarch of our entire family and the one to whom we all look for advice and support. You cannot imagine the admiration I have for you; I would not be half the woman I am without you.

I would be remiss if I didn't offer a special thanks to my dear friends Noel, Kathy, and Karen for their love and support. Each of you shared my grief along the way and always seemed to know just what I needed and when. You are amazing people and amazing friends, and I am so fortunate to have you in my life. Noel, a special thanks to you for always bringing me back to God, even when I strayed or doubted. Unlike me, you never wavered.

To my editor and friend, Bobbi Linkemer, simply knowing that God strategically placed you into my personal life was a continual reminder that I was destined to write this book. I am honored to know you and honored that you took the time (when you had little to give) to edit my manuscript.

Finally, I owe my life to my Lord and Savior, who carefully placed each of these people in my life as part of a masterful plan. While it took me many years to develop my relationship with Him, He will live forever in my heart and soul and drives each and every decision in my life. I will live forever in His grace and for His Glory.

INTRODUCTION

This book is intended to achieve one essential purpose: to bring hope into your heart, regardless of what difficulty you may be going through. The unimaginable pain I suffered after tragically losing my best friend, husband and soul mate was the inspiration and motivation for the words that follow. As I personally began the grieving process, I became somewhat obsessed with the notion that there must be an easier and more effective way to grieve. I realize how silly that sounds to most, but my overly logical mind believed that there had to be some method to expedite the process and thus I began a healing journey that ultimately resulted in this book.

While I was struggling with the loss of my husband, I became acutely aware of the pain in the world around us all. As I watched the nightly news I saw tragedy and pain daily, and my heart ached for the families who lost someone or something of importance or value. Often I cried for them. Seeing myself as a strong, willful, and capable person who hurt horribly from my own loss, I wondered how "those people" who were perhaps less equipped than I could get through it. "Not everyone is so tough," I thought, and here I was struggling immensely. To give you some idea of my thinking, I asked some friends and family to describe my character in five words or less. The two adjectives that came up several times were strong and courageous. So you see, I wondered, if the process was this difficult for me, how could I possibly make it easier for others?

As you will discover throughout this book, I learned that each of us is perfectly equipped to handle whatever tragedy enters into our life. It matters not what adjectives your friends would use to describe you. With that understanding, I also learned that coping begins with hope. If you do not have hope that you will heal from your pain, and hope that something good will result from it, your equipment will fail, you will fail, and the grief will consume you and your life.

I was told of a tragic story of a mother and father whose sixteen-year-old son was killed in a car accident by a drunk driver. Unfortunately, such things happen all too often. In a short version of the story, the mother, although suffering immense grief, locked her heart to God and her faith and always remained hopeful. The father did not. He turned to alcohol to numb his pain. The result was more pain, anger, resentment and bitterness, and eventually the marriage was broken. The father died only five years later, and many said he died of a broken heart. The mother, even after the divorce, held out hope that something good would come of her son's death and her pain. Finally it did. As she began to heal, she channeled her pain and energy into speaking to high school students about drunk driving, of course, using the death of her son as an example. She spoke at grief groups to parents who had lost children. She became an amazing advocate against drunk driving in her community. She could not have accomplished any of this if she hadn't experienced the pain of losing a child, but more importantly if she hadn't had hope that something good would come from it.

This book shares my story about finding the love of a lifetime, his battle with cancer, his tragic and unexpected death, and ultimately a new and loving relationship resulting from it all. That relationship is with God. Because I am not a biblical expert, you won't find quotes from scripture here, although you will feel the love of God come through. The only thing on which I consider myself an expert is my life, and that is what I am sharing with you. I hope that this book either helps you heal from a loss or prepares you for a time when you may suffer from one. You see, death is inevitable and cannot be avoided. Therefore, grief is inevitable.

This book is how I have chosen to "pay it forward."

The Love Story

One cold December night, I made the decision. We had argued about it for days and it was no longer up for debate. "You are going to the emergency room right now, or I will call an ambulance," I said. At that moment, my worst thought was that surgery might be necessary, but given my healthcare background, I thought to myself, "Surgery, no big deal." Never would I have dreamed this night was the beginning of the most tragic time in my life and that I would be forever changed by the events that followed. Strangely, that one night sparked the beginning of a new life and the tragic end of another.

Rob and I met in spring of 1994. In a loud and dimly lit country bar, this amazingly handsome man caught my attention. Since I was much to shy to approach him, I sent my gregarious girlfriend over to talk to him. Within a few moments, they both were approaching me. I can remember being incredibly nervous, so much so that I found myself speechless, something of a rarity for me. This would not be the last time Rob would leave me speechless. After being introduced and a few moments of breaking-the-ice awkwardness, we talked and danced the night away. When the night ended, Rob walked me to my car, opened my door, and gave me a goodbye kiss that could not be easily forgotten. As I drove home I felt incredibly excited, and I wondered if he would call me. I also felt exceedingly nervous about dating again.

The day after meeting Rob, I left my office and headed for home, anxious to see if he had called. This was long before the days of cell phones and texting. I arrived home, went straight to my answering machine and found nothing. Quickly I surmised that Rob was just another guy who said he would call but didn't. At the exact moment that I had that thought, the phone rang, and it was Rob! We talked for hours and much too late into the night. Over the next few months, we saw each other as often as possible and began falling in love; of this there was no doubt. Because we were becoming so close, Rob felt it was important to let me know that he had a four year old son. I was only in my early twenties and came from a broken home. I nearly panicked. How could I possibly help raise a child? How could I be a good stepparent when I didn't even want children of my own yet? As painful as it was, a few days after that, Rob and I agreed that our new relationship would have to end but that we would remain friends.

The years passed so quickly. I went off to college and then moved to Georgia to attend law school. Our friendship became less and less close as I suppose we should have expected. We kept up with each other's lives through mutual friends but rarely talked to each other, until May 23, 2003. The gregarious girlfriend who had introduced us at the bar was getting married in the Cayman Islands and hired Rob as her photographer. At that period in his life, Rob had proved to be an extremely talented photographer. I was the maid of honor. I thought to myself how nice it would be to see him again after all these years.

Another turning point in our lives happened at that four-day wedding. Rob attended with a date, as did I; however, the candid pictures tell the story all too well. Nearly every photo was of Rob and me together, not of us with our dates. Ironically, we were not even aware of this. After returning home to Georgia, I pondered why two people who seemed so drawn to each other were continually separated by life's circumstances.

Again, the years passed, but this time we stayed in contact, regularly. Rob became my sounding board for all my man troubles, and I began acting as his matchmaker. I offered up several friends of mine who I thought would suit Rob perfectly. Thankfully, I was a failure at matchmaking. It seemed like Rob and I were destined to be single the rest of our lives, an idea neither of us reveled in. And then what we refer to as "the wine night" happened. It had been a long, hard day at the law firm, so I thought a glass of wine would help me unwind. The glass of wine turned into a bottle as I contemplated life and all that seemed wrong with it. As anyone who has had a few too many knows, this is the time that you should never call someone, but of course you think everyone can't wait to talk to you. I called my good friend Rob. After all, who else would put up with me in this state?

Now, there was an ongoing dispute about what was *exactly* said that night, but eventually we agreed that I said, "When are you going to just come up here to Georgia and marry me?" And there it was. The feelings were out in the open again, but this time, neither Rob nor I were involved in a relationship. His son by this point had grown into a young man. Finally, the timing was right! After just a few conversations and a few visits, we were married on October 22, 2005, and moved together to Jacksonville, Florida. Our lives had come together again, and we couldn't have been happier. It was like a dream come true, a long-awaited fresh start. It was almost as if we had never been apart. Life couldn't have been better. We built a beautiful new home that we shared with our dog Samantha and two cats, Tux and Wahoo, which we referred to as our Fur Babies.

The excruciating wait in the emergency room was finally over. The x-rays were back, confirming that Rob had a blockage in his colon. The doctor's face told us more. We could see that this was not just a blockage; it was something far more sinister. As I probed the ER physician relentlessly, she finally divulged what we feared. She said with a troubled face, "There is a good chance this is a tumor," followed by a sheepish reassurance that the tumor could be benign. My heart almost beat out of my chest. I almost collapsed. How could this be? Rob was only

14

forty years old. He's too young for cancer. Rob said nothing for a while and then finally spoke. I will never forget those words. He said, "Baby, I knew I had cancer. I just somehow knew. Now, go home and get some sleep because this is going to be a long journey."

It was 3:00 in the morning on my drive home from the ER. My mind raced about the possibilities. I told myself over and over that the doctor was wrong. Once the surgeon removes the blockage or tumor or whatever it was, Rob will be fine. It can't be cancer. He has no family history. He's too young. It would be so unfair. I prayed. I remember apologizing to God for not praying for so long and for not going to church. I begged God to take me instead. "Give me Rob's cancer and let him live," I repeated over and over again. Knowing that wouldn't be done, I begged him to heal Rob and promised I would be a good Christian from now on. I was bartering with God.

I returned to the hospital three hours later when Rob was moved into a room. Sleep was out of the question. After several grueling hours of waiting to see a physician, the surgeon came in and confirmed that, in his opinion, the tumor was cancer and they would have to perform the surgery emergently, as soon as the operating room was available. The fear fully set in this time. Immediately, I wanted to know everything, and I mean *everything*, about the cancer—what type, the prognosis, and what treatment would be done following surgery. Of course, the surgeon could answer none of these questions until the tumor was removed and the pathology was back. Suddenly, my focus shifted to "I have to let his family know." Making those calls felt like the worst day of my life. At that moment, I never thought that making that call would be far easier than one I made four-and-a-half years later.

My mom, Dad, and Rob's mom were the first to arrive, followed by Rob's dad, who had to travel from California. My mom launched into soldier mode and propped me up emotionally. Rob's mom doted over him. The surgery took five hours, but the results seemed to only take five minutes. Rob had stage IIIC adenocarcinoma in his colon. He had eleven positive lymph nodes, not a good sign. The tumor had extended through the colon wall, another bad sign. The five-year survival rate for this advanced cancer was far worse than I could have imagined. Because the tumor was so large and his colon had stretched severely from the blockage, a colostomy had to be placed. Rob didn't know this yet because he was still in recovery. I dreaded his reaction. I dreaded meeting with the oncologist the following day. All I could do was comfort Rob the best I could and research non-stop to educate myself about this horrible disease.

Have you ever been wide-awake and yet you thought you must be dreaming? I felt that way for days on end. Rob's hospital stay lasted eleven days. He insisted that I stay with him overnight every night, an idea I secretly treasured. I didn't want to leave him. Unfortunately, the only place for me to sleep was in a blue plastic La-Z-Boy type chair. I am five feet tall and at that time probably barely weighed a hundred pounds. Each night I would pile into this chair and try desperately to recline. Occasionally I would succeed but only momentarily. Apparently I didn't weigh enough to keep it in the reclined position. This gave Rob a good laugh each night as I battled that ugly blue chair. Just about the time I would doze off it would slam shut, nearly throwing me on the floor. He compared it to the fact that I also didn't weigh enough to engage the passenger side airbag in his truck. Rob was six foot three, so you can picture us, the somewhat odd couple. Eventually, I learned to sleep curled up in a ball with my head hanging over the arm of that ugly blue chair. It mattered little, since there was no chance of sleeping well anyway. Rob was still vomiting regularly, and the nurses were in and out all night. The alarms seemed relentless. On occasion, Rob would convince me to crawl into bed with him, carefully working around all the IV lines.

On the last day of the hospital stay, an ostomy nurse taught us how to clean and change the colostomy bag. I listened intently. I tried to remember each step. Rob fully disengaged. He wanted nothing to do with this bag attached to his body. I think it was a sort of denial, and I couldn't blame him. It didn't matter to me since I had already decided Rob's only job was to fight cancer, and I would do everything else. Given that I had not left the hospital in eleven days, my brain was tired, and trying to learn all the steps was daunting. Nevertheless, I was fairly sure I had it down pat. Regardless, we would receive only that one visit from an ostomy nurse.

The oncologist finally came for the last visit and confirmed the chemotherapy plan, which would begin in a few weeks. All I could focus on was taking my husband home. I wanted him out of that place where the "sick people" were. I thought that I could take better care of him at home. I wanted to lie next to him in the bed and hold him for the first time in now eleven days.

Sometime around 3:00 AM the first day home, Rob woke me and said, "What's that smell?" I looked all around the floor thinking one of our pets had an accident but couldn't find anything. Wait, could it be the colostomy bag? And so it was. We hadn't had one night of sleep yet and our first test began. It took both of us working together to recall the steps about how to change the darn thing. Through our sleepy stupor, it took us an hour. We agreed that it should not be this hard and hoped the home health ostomy nurse could explain it better when she came.

The next day and evening came and went fairly uneventfully. Rob was still having some fairly intense surgical pain and was therefore still taking narcotics. I tell you this because of what happened that night. He had gone to bed for the evening. I lay with him until he drifted off to sleep. I couldn't sleep no matter how hard I tried. I had so much to learn about cancer and spent most of the nights doing

18

research. That evening my learning was interrupted by a phone call. It was my dear friend Kathy from whom I had gotten Samantha (my dog) about eleven years before. I hadn't told her the news yet. She had an excitement in her voice and couldn't wait to tell me something. I thought, maybe it would be nice to talk about something besides cancer, so I let her carry on without interrupting to share the bad news.

Rob and I had pondered for some time whether to get another dog, a friend for Samantha. She was getting older, so we always hesitated. We worried a puppy would be too much for her to handle. Coincidentally, that night Kathy blurted out, "You will never believe it! I have a puppy for you." She went on to explain that a litter of Sheltie puppies had been born in Jacksonville only a few miles from us and that she had already put in a good word with the breeder for me. Eventually, I was able to cut into the conversation, and I began to cry. I told Kathy what we had been going through, and I believe she was in shock for a moment or two. Then, in perfect Kathy fashion, she began to reason why a puppy would be perfect during this difficult time. A puppy would bring joy and laughter among the pain and sadness. Although this made some sense, I just couldn't imagine having to raise a pup at this time. The getting up in the middle of the night for pee breaks was tiring normally, and I felt that I hadn't slept for weeks as it was.

Finally I retired to bed. Rob woke up as I cuddled up next to him. He said, "I heard you on the phone. Who were you talking to?" I replied briefly, "Kathy." He asked what she wanted, and I told him about the litter of pups. Never in my wildest dreams would I have guessed what would come next. Rob turned the light on, hugged me and said, "Let's get two!" I laughed at him and told him that must be the drugs talking. "Go back to sleep."

The next morning we decided to get one puppy, not two. It was a compromise. Rob couldn't wait to pick out his new puppy. He chose a tiny and sweet little girl whom he named Izabella, Izzy for short. When she was old enough to come home I realized Kathy had been right. This was just what Rob needed. She slept next to him constantly, sometimes on his neck, sometimes on his shoulders, but always nearby. Izzy seemed to always understand that she belonged to Rob and that she served some very special purpose. We called her his therapy dog. Izzy's coming to live with us was the first time we learned we could love cancer in some strange sort of way. Our understanding of loving cancer became deeper as time passed. Of course, I was exhausted with the house training process, but it was to be expected. She and Rob were worth it.

The next week was the one-week follow up with the surgeon. Expecting nothing more than a peek at the wound and maybe getting the staples out, we were shocked when the doctor informed us that the wound was infected and was not healing. It would have to be reopened and left open until it healed from the inside out. This would require special dressing changes three times a day and eventually the use of a device called a wound V.A.C. My head was spinning. Rob refused to speak. How can this be happening? This can't be real. Chemotherapy would have to be postponed until the wound healed. This concerned me deeply but there was nothing more that could be done. Chemotherapy would cause the wound not to heal and would increase the risk of infection, so it had to wait.

The surgeon scheduled a time to have the wound opened and debrided (removal of dead tissue) and Rob's port-a-cath placed; this would be used to administer chemotherapy. Considering all that had happed, Rob worried about something unexpected occurring during surgery. On the other hand, I was very positive and somewhat unconcerned about the idea of the wound being left open.

As far back as I can remember and until about the age of fourteen, my family lived on a small farm. At any given time we would have horses, cattle, pigs, dogs, cats and any wounded wild animal that came along needing our help. Over the years, I watched in awe as the vets stitched up wounds, castrated bulls and stallions, and administered routine care. Admittedly, I would feel a little woozy during the castrations, but it was likely out of sympathy more so than the sight of it. Given my upbringing, I was certain nothing the surgeon would do to Rob's wound would bother me.

The surgeon finally came to the surgery waiting room and took me to the consult area. To my relief, he explained the surgery had gone exactly as planned. He explained the extensive after-care Rob would require, and I worried about taking that much time off from my work. Rob came home the same day after spending some time in recovery. The next day, the home health nurse arrived to teach me how to dress the wound. I was anxious and ready to learn. I insisted that Rob should not look at the wound. Nothing good could come from seeing it. I put a ball cap over his head so he couldn't peek and talked to him to keep his mind off of what was happening.

I wrote down each step. First, the nurse unwrapped the top of the dressing. Then, she began pulling hunks of gauze out of the wound. I couldn't understand how that much gauze was inside the wound. When all the gauze was removed, I was shocked. The wound was much wider and much deeper than I had imagined. As I stared at this gaping hole about ten inches long, I remember thinking, "My fist can fit in there." My mind raced and settled on the fact Rob had no idea what it looked like. I knew I couldn't let him see fear in my face, so I cracked jokes while the nurse worked at re-packing the wound with moist dressings. I could never understand why Rob said the dressing changes didn't hurt, but I believed it was in part because he never saw its ugliness until it was nothing more than a scar.

After months of daily wet-to-dry dressings and a few weeks on the Wound V.A.C. (a device that created suction inside the wound to expedite tissue healing), the wound was finally healed. The thought of chemo was daunting, but somehow we embraced it as the light at the end of the tunnel, the last step. Rob went on to complete six months of chemotherapy. The side effects were typical and expected. His blood counts remained good throughout the entire six months of treatment, and the oncologists were very pleased. Rob had been otherwise a very healthy and strong man before cancer, a fact that contributed to his successful completion of a very aggressive chemo regimen.

A few months after the last chemo treatment, life seemed to return to normal. Well, by normal I mean that Rob was now living each day as a cancer survivor. Normal existed, but only between frequent blood work and PET scans. Eventually, the colostomy (yes, yet another surgery) was reversed and his port-a-cath removed, allowing Rob to truly feel that this horrible experience was over for good. Both of us returned to work and to our normal lives. We desperately tried to forget about cancer. Despite a bit of skepticism, I chose to believe that Rob was cured; I had long ago forgotten my bartered promise to God.

One year passed, two years passed, and no cancer. The doctors were very pleased and seemed quite positive about how he was doing. Rob and I never quite knew what to feel. We remained positive, but it was if this little shred of doubt lingered in a haunting way. We rarely discussed the possibility of the cancer recurring. The prognosis statistics were not in Rob's favor, but I simply refused to focus on that fact. Rob had adamantly refused to know the survival rate statistics, but I knew. Sometimes I wished I didn't.

During the summer of 2009, the CEA (blood work) began to rise, a possible indication that the cancer had recurred. It rose very slowly at first but remained within normal ranges. The fear was hard to ignore. Two blood tests later over the next two months proved that the CEA was continuing to climb; the last test showed that the CEA level had reached an abnormal level, albeit only slightly outside the range. The doctors spoke to me on the phone and tried to reassure me that this elevation could be caused by something other than cancer recurrence. Nevertheless, the doctors immediately performed additional highly sensitive blood tests and another PET/CT scan. Nothing was found. Feeling some relief, neither Rob nor I felt totally confident with the negative results.

Once again, I began staying up late into the night researching what other condition could cause the CEA to elevate to abnormal levels. Finally, I found it! Rob had been experiencing significant joint pain for months. His primary care physician said it was gout, a diagnosis I didn't agree with. To me, the symptoms were not consistent with gout, and the medications did not help. Finally, my research revealed that Rob was suffering from psoriatic arthritis, and more

24

importantly, there were clinical studies showing a correlation between this disease and elevated CEA levels. At the next oncologist visit, we discussed my findings with the head physician. The oncologist only half-heartedly agreed but did recommend that Rob see a rheumatologist. The rheumatologist confirmed that Rob had psoriatic arthritis. Sadly, the treatment to relieve his intense pain could not be used, as that medication increased the risk of developing cancer. We left knowing that Rob would continue to be in pain but that maybe the CEA was high due to this new disease rather than to cancer. Unfortunately, month after month, the CEA continued to rise until finally, in October 2009, the scan revealed a mass in Rob's abdomen.

For those of you reading this who may have cancer or have a loved one who has cancer, you are probably thinking this book is a downer. Well, at this point I would agree, so let me tell you now that Rob did not die of cancer. There is happiness and humor that came from this all, but before we get to that, the real tragedy must be revealed.

The week after Rob was diagnosed with recurrent cancer, I lost my job. Like so many people, we needed two incomes in order to pay the bills. Again, I asked, how could this be happening? I quit praying and became angry with God. I began to even wonder if there was a God. How could He do this? Why? We are good people and we didn't deserve this. My big sister (and friend) stepped in to remove our financial worries, and I shifted my focus away from losing my job and focused once again on helping Rob.

Rob had another major abdominal surgery to remove the new tumor. We spent another eleven days in the hospital much like before. This time, however, Rob did not require a colostomy bag, something he adamantly refused to undergo again. Once he healed from the surgery, the oncologists determined what chemo regimen would be done this time. The doctors insisted that the treatments would have to be aggressive because they believed there was still a chance to cure Rob. Newer and more specialized medications were now available for those with recurrent colon cancer. Essentially, the doctors explained that if a cure didn't happen this time, the cancer would be deemed incurable. I heard terminal. Rob agreed to be as aggressive as possible. He told the doctors he wanted to live but that if it didn't work this time, he would not go through chemo again.

The chemo regimen was very different this time, and the reactions were extremely harsh. Rob experienced extreme esophageal pain for days following each treatment, and after the second treatment, he developed a serious and painful rash reaction. The doctors were forced to discontinue the specialized medicine. Rob was relieved to have that drug removed from the regimen but I was terrified. If he couldn't tolerate the high doses and new medicines, his chances for cure were lessened.

Whatever the case, Rob needed my support now more than ever. Unbelievably, during one of the worst of the treatments, my beloved dog of thirteen years was dying. Her kidneys were failing. Rob was writhing in pain, and I could see that Samantha was rapidly declining. I wanted to cry, but there was no time. I rushed her to the vet and told Rob I would be right back. I had called ahead to the vet and explained my situation. He and his staff had everything ready to go so that I could be expedited in and out as quickly as possible.

The vet insisted that I treat Samantha with subcutaneous fluids at home for a week and that she would be fine for another few months. He insisted with all that was going on, now was not the time to put her down. I agreed, but now I had to care for two. I was fractured emotionally and physically. When I returned home, Rob's pain had worsened, and I believed we would have to go to the emergency room. I called the oncologist and was waiting for the return call with instruction. Samantha needed her fluids. Feeling completely helpless with both of them sick, I called a friend who was a neonatal nurse and essentially begged for help. I needed her to take over Samantha's care. Certainly, with her nursing background, she could administer the fluids. This was the first time I had asked for help, and for once, my stupid pride didn't matter. I was so thankful for her rescue that evening.

That night passed without a trip to the ER, but the treatments didn't get better. Rob and the oncologist finally agreed he would have to use strong narcotics to manage the pain, a concept Rob hated. During his first round of chemo the doctor had given him a narcotic. When the pain started, I would fuss at Rob and say, "Take the darn medicine. That's what it's for." The medicine never seemed to help much and one day, I discovered why. Rob was squirreling the pills away in his belly button because he didn't like the way the pills made him feel. Of course, this made me laugh, and I stopped harping on him. I loved telling this story to people who came to visit because it helped us all to learn how to laugh again. This round of chemo, however, Rob took the medicine around the clock without any prompting, which told me the pain had to be severe.

Rob had treatments every two weeks and eventually found ways to manage the side effects somewhat better. In December, Samantha went into full kidney failure. Her time had come, and together we made the agonizing decision to put her to sleep. My heart felt broken, but I had to stay strong to get Rob through the final rounds of chemo. Less than a month later, an ironic phone call came. Rob had only been in chemo a few weeks and my friend Kathy called to tell me that another litter of Sheltie puppies had been born.

Just as before, I thought bringing a new puppy into our home during this time would be too much. Besides, my feelings about Samantha's death were still so raw. Once again, Kathy found all the right reasons why we needed some new love and happiness in our home. I still hesitated until I began to notice that Izzy was grieving badly. She clearly missed her friend Samantha. We all missed her. In January, Spencer joined our family; he was our first male Sheltie and he was our second "cancer therapy" dog. Just as Izabella had done, Spencer and his puppy antics brought us many laughs, and his insatiable desire for cuddling was much needed.

Rob finished chemo in May 2010, and it felt like relief at last for both of us. During the last round of chemo, Rob had shared with me again that he would not do any more treatments if the cancer recurred. As hard as it was, I understood and supported his decision. I thought about the possibility of his life ending in the near future. I constantly wondered what I could do to make him see how important he was on this earth and to so many people. I wanted him to know what a difference he made in people's lives. I wanted him to know how special he was. I decided these would be the things he would want to know and think about when his life was coming to an end. Don't we all want to know that we mattered? I wanted him to have peace when his time came to cross over. As I pondered what to do, I thought much about what really mattered in our last days on earth.

Finally, I decided a huge party was in order. With Kathy's help, the planning began. We aimed to throw Rob a huge surprise party to celebrate his life. Kathy, who is far more techy than I, developed a website with photos of his journey through cancer and used it to invite friends and family. I arranged for a huge tent, a band, and catered food. It was proving to be huge success. The number of RSVPs was overwhelming. People were planning to fly in from California and were coming from all over the state. My heart was happy. The party would be July 24, 2010.

Just like that night in the emergency room where it all began, I could have never dreamed that this date would tragically change my life. This time even more.

ALL GOOD THINGS MUST END

Later you will learn much more about the person Rob was, but suffice to say, he loved life. Since cancer has a way of teaching you to appreciate every single minute of life, it is no surprise that the two (Rob and cancer) collided. Rob once said that cancer had been a gift to us and after some explaining, I agreed. It forced our life into perspective. We vacationed more instead of making excuses about the cost. We loved harder, we spent time with friends and family, and we planned ahead in case one of us was to die.

Cancer also has a way of making you fulfill your dreams. One of Rob's dreams was to have a sport bike. I hated the idea of him riding a motorcycle, especially that type, but what was I to do? I understood his need to live and enjoy life. Rob was focused on his bucket list. We both understood the likelihood that he would succumb to cancer eventually. After much discussion about why riding a sport bike was a bad idea, Rob bought the bike and couldn't wait to hit the road. We agreed to spare no expense on having all the proper and best quality safety gear, and Rob agreed to wear his gear at all times.

Rob also dreamed about riding his bike at "the dragon." For those who may not know, this is a treacherous mountain area that draws bikers from all over the country. So it came to be. On July 14 Rob and a friend headed to the mountains with their bikes. I had had fought him many times about going to this area because of the danger involved, but I lost the battle this time. He wanted to go so badly that he decided to go against my will. There really was no way of stopping him this time. When I kissed him goodbye and told him, I loved him I confessed that he had to come home because I had planned a party for him. He smiled and said, "You can't ever keep a surprise, Julie." He was right about that, but this time I told him for a different reason. There was something inside me that made me think, "What if the worst happened and he never even knew about the party?" I didn't tell him of the magnitude of the party. I at least kept that much a surprise. I wish I hadn't.

When we talked on the phone the next night, I reminded him that he had to come home for the party. Again, I had this haunting feeling that something bad was going to happen. Reminding him of the party was my way, I guess, of telling him I was scared about him being there. I will never forget the words that followed: "Baby, if I don't make it back, it will make for a nice wake." He giggled, obviously intending to make a joke. I didn't laugh, and I didn't think it was funny.

The next day, as I was performing my morning animal feedings, I noticed a large growth on our cat's head. My heart sank and another bad feeling came across me, giving me chills. I wondered if I should wait until Rob came home to take him to the veterinarian in case it was serious. I didn't want to deal with losing another animal, and I certainly didn't want to have to go through it alone. As I pondered what to do for a while, I rubbed Wahoo's little head until something finally told me that it couldn't wait. Thankfully, my dear friend Karen had the time to go with me. I remember telling her that I thought Wahoo probably had cancer. Somehow I just knew.

The vet took Wahoo in the back to draw off some cells from the swollen area in order to make a diagnosis. When she left the room, I told Karen again, "It's cancer." Karen told me to be positive and not to think the worst, but it didn't matter. I had seen that look on a doctor's face before. I had heard doctors provide reassurance verbally in the past with Rob, but at the same time, their body language sent a different message. Finally, when the vet returned with Wahoo, she explained it was an aggressive type of cancer and that, ultimately, it would be a quick but likely painful death. My fears had come true, and I began to sob. With Rob away, I decided to put our dear cat of sixteen years to sleep. I didn't want him to suffer. I was inconsolably upset when I returned home alone. I worried even more that day about Rob being on the bike in the mountains. I had now lost two of my animals, and I was obsessed with the idea that something was going to happen to Rob. That evening I told a friend, "I feel like Wahoo's death is somehow supposed to prepare me for Rob's death." It seemed like a silly thing to say, but for some reason I felt compelled to say it.

Rob finally called that evening, and we began arguing about everything. I told him about Wahoo and cried again. I was mad at him for not being with me when Wahoo died regardless of the fact that he couldn't have been. I was being horribly unreasonable about everything, and I knew it, but I couldn't stop myself. I wanted him home and that was that. Nothing he could say would make me happy at this point. We talked for hours and finally decided there was no need to continue arguing over nothing. I was being unreasonable, and nothing good would come of it. I told him I loved him and to please be careful up there. He said, "I love you to the moon and back, baby. See you Sunday."

Saturday came. All day I was anxious to talk to Rob. I hated that we had argued, and I hated that his cell phone wouldn't work in the mountains. The day seemed to pass so slowly as I waited for him to return to the hotel after his ride and call me.

Around 4:00 PM on July 17, I had the second spiritual experience of my life. The first had been many years ago when an uncle had passed unexpectedly. Within moments of waking from a dream about my uncle dying, the phone rang and my aunt confirmed that he had died that night. It was an event in my life that I never forgot, not even one single detail.

I didn't know yet why, but I had this sudden and overwhelming thought that Rob was never coming home. It was much stronger than the worry that had been haunting me for days. My heart raced, and I could not change my own mind. I could not convince myself that what I was feeling was nothing more than pointless worry. Later, I learned that this feeling occurred at the time of his death, almost exactly.

It was only 4:00 in the afternoon and much too early to expect a call from him. Nevertheless, I was absolutely panicking. I called his cell phone repeatedly, knowing it wouldn't work in the mountains. I told myself to stop worrying, since he would not be able to call until they returned to the hotel around 6:00 PM. It didn't matter. I knew something was wrong, and my logical brain could not convince me otherwise. Still, I clung to the hope that, come Sunday when he returned home, all my anguish would be over and I would feel silly about the needless worry.

Around 5:00 PM that evening I called my good friend Noel who is what I refer to as "spiritually connected." I thought surely she would not think I was crazy if I told her what I was feeling. I also remembered that two weeks before I had felt the need to ask her if she had any feelings about when Rob would pass. At the time, I thought my line of questioning stemmed from his battles with cancer. I had never felt compelled to ask her that question before. Now, it seemed like a premonition.

Noel obliged me that evening and came over to wait for the call from Rob with me. We laughed a little while her kids played in the pool and I was happy for the slight distraction from my thinking. The time seemed to pass so slowly. As it passed, there was still no call from Rob. By 6:00 PM I told my friend that I was convinced something had happened to Rob. More time passed. I wanted to make excuses for why he hadn't called, but I couldn't. No matter what, Rob would call to let me know he was all right. Something was horribly wrong. I knew it in every place of my being and I had no way to find out. As day turned into night, my worry developed into full-blown hysteria.

At 10:00 PM, there was a knock on the door, and in front of me stood a police officer. I will never forget that moment. He never had to speak because I already knew. Rob had been killed on the motorcycle. I dropped to my knees. Not to pray, mind you. That was the last thing on my mind. No loving God would do this. I wanted to die, and I wanted to die right then. Finally, I allowed the police officer to speak, and he told me even more horrible news. Rob had crashed into three other bikers and at least two were injured, but thankfully their injuries were not fatal. I was relieved that they had survived and felt empathy for their families and wives who would be thrust into the caregiver role I had come to know so well. I knew all too well how difficult that could be. From that moment forward, there are many gaps in my memory of that night, but I will share what I do recall.

For a short moment my mind wondered. Had Rob planned this? Is that why he said, "It would make for a nice wake"? Was this his way of not having to deal with the possibility of cancer recurring? These thoughts rushed quickly through my mind and then, almost immediately, left for good, never to be entertained again. I knew two things about Rob that could not be doubted, ever. Rob would never have done something intentional that could even possibly result in someone else being hurt. He simply couldn't hurt another person. He had spent his entire life helping others. I almost laughed for a moment when I thought, he could have just have easily wrecked avoiding a squirrel. The other thing I knew was this: Rob loved me far too much to have left that way knowing the pain it would cause. More importantly, Rob didn't even know yet if the chemo had worked or not. He might have been cured. We will never know the answer to that question, of course. It was settled. This was a tragic accident, by the very definition of the word. I never questioned that fact again.

Remember when I told you how hard it was to call his parents to inform them of the cancer? Imagine now having to make this call. I had to call his mother and father and tell them Rob had died. Even worse, Rob and I had lied to his father about having the motorcycle because we knew how his father would worry. His father didn't even know the bike existed. Rob would hide it at the neighbor's when his father came to visit. The calls were made, and his parents (and mine) began making travel arrangements immediately. For a moment, it seemed all I had to do now was cry. I was incredibly mistaken.

Sometime very late into the night, I remembered that a hundred or so people were planning to come to our house for a party in Rob's honor the following Saturday, in just seven days. I realized that I had to tell them all, too. All I could think was, "This can't be real." This cannot be happening. Even worse, it seemed I had to keep reliving it by having to repeat it over and over. As my friends and family heard the news, they rallied around and began informing everyone they could so I had less to handle in that regard.

Over the period of years during Rob's illness, I came to believe that praying didn't matter. God never listened, at least not to me. Now, He had taken my dog, my cat, and now Rob, unexpectedly and most unfairly. Anger with God was an understatement. I wondered what Rob or I or both had done to deserve such a harsh and unfair life. Was this punishment for some wrong we had committed? Ironically, as much as I wanted not to believe in or even think about God, there the thoughts were. They were not nice thoughts, but somehow God was still in my head.

The night passed and I watched the sun rise. I never fell asleep that night. I couldn't. As morning came, our house became filled with people pouring out love and support and, of course, food. People came from all over. They grabbed whatever task that needed to be done and did it. All I could think about was the obituary and eulogy I had to write. You see, Rob and I talked about the day of his death. I told him time and again that I couldn't bear standing up and giving his eulogy because it would hurt too badly. I told him I would freeze up and wouldn't be able to speak. Rob, time and again, would laugh at me and say, "You will do fine. You always have something to say, Julie." While I'm known for being a big talker, do you recall my telling you that Rob often left me speechless? Here I was again, having to stand up and give his eulogy, and no words would come. Regardless, the time had come to do it and I simply couldn't let Rob down. I had to do this for him. It seemed to be my last chance to make him proud.

While I was not yet aware of what was happening, my life-altering change and reason for this book was beginning to unfold. Amidst the chaos, I also had to decide what type of funeral or memorial to have for Rob. He had always jokingly said about cancer, "Just have a big party when I die." I hated when he said that, but I pretended to understand. The words he said to me during our phone call that weekend haunted me. "...[the party] will make for a nice wake, baby." I wondered now, did Rob have some sense of intuitive knowing like I did? How could this have come to be? I had planned a party on the date that would now become his memorial. I had planned this party three months before his death. Everyone already had arranged flights and hotels to be here.

It was some months later when I heard an eerie and somewhat similar story on the local news. A police officer's young son had asked him out of the blue one day, "Dad, what would you do if someone broke into our house?" I surmised he probably thought about such things either because of something he had seen on television or simply because his father was a police officer. Whatever the case, the father replied to his son, "I would die to protect my family, son." Ironically, or perhaps not so ironically, a short time thereafter, the family fell victim to a home invasion. After a gunfight between the officer and the two men who broke in, everyone except the mother and the child were killed. The officer literally did exactly as he had promised; he had protected his family and lost his own life. Listening to this story, chills rushed throughout my body. Did this young son and his father have some sense of knowing of what was about to happen? While this was an entirely different story, it seemed so much the same to me at that moment.

Although Rob had jokingly said, "Have a big party when I die," a party was out of the question. Nevertheless, I knew that his memorial had to be special and as upbeat as possible. Rob wouldn't want sadness and pain. He had told me so. Again, I couldn't let him down. My mind raced back to the eulogy. Whatever I wrote had to be positive and had to somehow help to ease the pain of those who would mourn him. Because some might wonder what I finally came to say that day, I have included his eulogy in the appendix of this book.

As I pondered what type of service to have, I couldn't bear the thought of it being at a funeral home. The only funerals I had attended at my young age had been elderly people, and they were all held at funeral homes. Rob wasn't old, and I wasn't old, and a funeral home memorial just didn't seem right. It felt almost creepy. Nonetheless, I didn't know where else it could be done on such short notice. I kept coming back to the idea that I would have it in a church, but Rob and I didn't have a church. We had talked about going to a church close to us but never did. We wanted to have God in our lives, but we had essentially given up on Him since He had seemingly given up on us. Finally, after much thought, I decided a memorial at a church was the only option, but what church would accept us?

Enter the picture, an angel here on earth. Within less than a day of telling my friends and family that I wanted a memorial service to be held in a church, a neighbor and now a good friend arranged for us to use the nearby church, the pastor to speak, the church atrium to be decorated, food to be delivered, and people to serve the memorial attendees. I was stunned beyond belief. I could not believe a church would do this for someone they never even met. This open-arms welcome by the church and its family was the beginning of a new life for me. Ultimately, it is the reason for this book, as you will later fully understand. Amazingly, had this one act of kindness not occurred, my life would be unbearably different.

LAUGHING AT CANCER

Reviewing our short years together, it would have been easy for Rob and I to become disheartened, callous, and defeated. At times, we did, but Rob refused to let those times last for long. Without my knowing, he decided to find ways to laugh at cancer. I soon learned to laugh along with him.

Rob was a notorious practical joker and so enjoyed making others laugh. He refused to allow cancer to subdue this part of him in any way. The first of many "cancer pranks" he pulled was while he was in the hospital just one day after his first surgery. I was driving home from the hospital to take a shower when I heard my cell phone ping notifying me of an incoming text message. Immediately, I looked down to see if it was Rob for fear something was wrong and I needed to turn around and go back. Much to my surprise, it was a photo of his "family jewels" with the Foley catheter in place. The accompanying text said, "Look baby, I can plug it in now to charge it up." You see, Rob would do anything to make me laugh and keep me strong through it all. Well, as you can imagine, I had to pull the car over and laugh until my belly hurt. All I could think was, I should have taken his cell phone away before I left. No telling what trouble he will get into while I'm gone. I felt a little sorry for his nurses that evening.

Again in an attempt to laugh at cancer, Rob pulled another hilarious stunt. I had gone outside to the patio one evening to talk to my sister on the phone. I was not aware that Rob was inside and up to no good. After a while I realized he had been awfully quiet for a long while. It was like a mother worrying what the children had gotten into. It was simply too quiet. My curiosity got the better of me, and I went in to see what he was up to. Picture the scene. Rob was in the kitchen with the Food Saver out, about twenty colostomy bags and a pair of scissors. I asked, "What in the world are you doing?" Rob, without hesitation, answered, "I'm making us some intimacy bags." I looked at his little masterpieces first in awe, and then the laughter began. He had made tiny colostomy bags, and sealed them with the Food Saver, giving each one a different shape. One was even shaped like a heart, my favorite, of course. One was round and had a smiley face drawn on it with a Sharpie. "Only Rob" was all I could think, as I laughed. I couldn't have been more proud of my genius. OK, maybe not really a genius, but if something didn't work the way Rob wanted, he would simply modify it or make it himself to meet his standards. There simply wasn't anything he couldn't do. We laughed together for a while as he continued to make these little bags. After he had made about fifteen of them, I asked, "Just how often do you think we are going to need these intimacy bags anyway?" We laughed for hours. This was the night we shook hands in agreement (a pact of sorts) that we would always find a way to laugh at cancer.

During the second bout of cancer, I created a blog site in order to keep friends and family abreast of Rob's progress. It proved to be a spectacular idea. Encouraging words came from all over. Of course, Rob promptly found a way to utilize the blog to spread his humor around the world. One post referred to the use of hair gel to keep his hair attached to his head rather than using it for styling. The chemo, of course, caused hair loss. Another post was used to request a supply of toilet paper and Lysol to be sent to me. The chemo had some rather bad side effects; hence, his silly request. During one treatment Rob had a severe allergic reaction to a new medication that caused his lips, nose, and ears to swell enormously, so Rob began referring to himself as Hitch (from the movie).

Naturally, once Rob's humorous posts began, so did those of his friends. This one bears repeating. A long-time friend of Rob's wrote, and I quote, "When people are talking about snow boarding I tell them about standing in a ski lift line with a friend [Rob] and his teenage son. This friend asks me 'do you know why I don't snowboard?' I reply, 'No.' My friend [Rob] smiles and gives his son a little shove. His son falls on his ass and [Rob] calmly says, 'Because you spend most of the day sitting in the snow.'" I wasn't there, but I can certainly picture Rob pulling that one.

44

When Rob returned to work at Home Depot, he couldn't wait to be back to his old tricks there, either. As Rob explained to me, his manager at the time was a bit of Christmas scrooge. This, of course, made him a target for Rob. When the manager had a day off, Rob, with the help of some handpicked employees, built an entire Santa's workshop in the his office. Rob and his cohorts in crime disassembled a shed from outside and reassembled it in the office. He moved a Christmas tree into the office and decorated every inch of the room. It took most of the day but in the end the office looked exactly like Santa's workshop. The pictures were hysterical, and his manager was duly impressed with Rob's joke. Rob had pulled other such pranks at work, but Santa's workshop proved to be the best practical joke thus far.

Another memory of Rob and his antics occurred just a month or so following his first abdominal surgery to remove the tumor. We decided to ride our bikes around the neighborhood and visit our friends along the way. It was a weekend, so most folks were out piddling in their yards and such. It took us a few hours to go just about a mile due to all the stops and chatting, but we had a wonderful time. As we rounded the corner for home, Rob spouted those famous last words, "Hey, watch this." Having no idea what he was about to do, I yelled from behind, "Don't you do it!" Seconds later, he attempted some bike trick involving spinning the handlebars around. All I really know is that he went splat right in front of me and I nearly ran him over. I panicked, thinking he could have injured his barely healed surgical wound. Fortunately, he was fine except for some pretty nasty road rash. I, on the other hand, nearly suffered a heart attack!

Through it all, Rob and I learned that sometimes life is so unfair and painful that the only thing you can do is laugh your way through it. That's not to say that we didn't have down moments. We did. That's not to say that sometimes you don't just break down and cry. We did. We were human after all, but one of us would always pull the other one back into laughter and positivity. If Rob were writing this instead of me, he would say to the world, "Just laugh at cancer. It beats the alternative."

SPIRITUAL AWAKENING

Up until the point of the motorcycle accident, I had Rob to lean on during the hard times. We got through the pain and the struggles together. Together, we could endure anything. The first week after his death, I lay in bed thinking about it all. I didn't eat. I rarely slept. I avoided everyone because I couldn't bear to hear another stupid cliché that was well intended but typically infuriated me. Seriously, I could write an entire book on the stupid things people unintentionally say when someone dies. The only activity I did on a daily basis was cry. Pain was my existence, and I doubted it would ever get better. I refused to pray. What was the point? I would only pray for Rob to be returned to me, which clearly would go unanswered like all the other prayers I said. I wanted to pray for my own death but didn't bother. I doubted that prayer would be answered either, and in reality it seemed a selfish request.

At some point during the following week, I decided that the only thing that could lessen my pain was to know that Rob existed in another world, on another plane, somewhere outside this earth. That is, I decided that I had to believe in heaven. I had to believe in God and his son, Jesus Christ. If I didn't, then Rob was completely dead, both body and soul. I had to believe that Rob had gone to heaven and that someday we would be reunited. In Rob's words, "It beats the alternative." But how could I believe this now? I had become a skeptic and a cynic. What could possibly change me now?

Almost as if a couple of friends read my mind, that day I received books in the mail and at my door. There were a total of six books given to me, all of which dealt in some way with life after death and spirituality. This was the first day I was able to stop crying. I was far too busy reading these books. I read one right after another. I took notes. I compared what the authors wrote, especially the concepts, ideas, or events that overlapped. Finally, I had hope and a belief that Rob's soul lived on. I even accepted that God existed and that Rob was with him in heaven. I decided I would work out why God had allowed all this to happen at a later date. Right now, I needed to know Rob was spiritually alive, and I wanted to know how to communicate with him. I believed I could do this since twice before I had some sense of knowing a death had occurred. I believed I must have some natural, innate ability to communicate with the spirit world. If I could communicate with Rob in the afterlife then I would know for sure, without any doubt whatsoever, that his soul lived on, I would be able to let him go with a knowing that we would be reunited some day. My spiritual journey had begun.

As I studied the books given to me, I learned many ways to communicate with the spirit world. Let me be very clear. It is not my intent in writing this book to share how this is done. It is not my intent to even condone it. In fact, I made a promise to myself and to God that if he would allow me tangible proof of Rob's existence, I would never attempt to communicate with the spirit world again. I had many reservations about doing so and I still do. Whatever the case, there I was, bartering with God again. I did, however, remember this promise and held to it.

All the skeptics and naysayers who read this will find earthly, human reasons for how or why things happened to me as they did. Believe as you wish. I know the truth, and I hope that those who need to know as I did find peace in what I am about to share.

Just a few days after beginning to read the books given to me, the first experience happened. In the early morning hours while I was sleeping, I heard the house phone ring, and I rolled over in bed and picked it up. I said hello in a half-awake sounding voice, and Rob said to me, "I'm OK, baby. I love you, but I have to go now." Before I could say anything back, I had a dial tone. I sat straight up in bed, shocked, happy, sad, and excited all at the same time. I wanted more. I knew that everyone would tell me I was dreaming. I knew I wasn't. I was wide awake.

Days passed and I kept reading and studying. One evening as I was reading feverishly, my spiritually connected friend, Noel, called and said she needed to come over. She said it was important and pleaded for a short visit with me. I conceded even though I wasn't much interested in company. I was lying in bed as usual. She snuggled up next to me and offered a warm hug. And then she quietly and calmly said, "I have something to tell you. Rob came to me when I was in prayer. I don't know what this means, and I don't want to know, but he wants you to forgive him." I began crying uncontrollably, thanked her, and, shortly thereafter asked her to leave. I lay there thinking about the foolish argument Rob and I had that night before he passed. I wanted Rob to forgive *me*, not the other way around! I felt incredibly guilty that perhaps he still felt bad about that night. Well, at least that was all I could surmise he meant. After much thought and many tears, it became even clearer that I had to communicate, somehow. He had to know how sorry I was. He had to know how much I loved and missed him.

I meditated regularly and began to notice things happening around me that I would likely never have noticed before. Often these things would happen when I was trying to communicate with Rob. Simple things, such as a rainbow appearing over my house (and only my house), two butterflies flying in tandem, and lights flickering without explanation now seemed so surreal.

In fact, looking back there seemed to have been communication from Rob only a day after his death. That night there was several people sitting outside telling stories about Rob, laughing and reminiscing. One of Rob's friends known for his unusual ability to rap like Eminem was there to "perform" one last time in Rob's honor. Strange as it was, we were having a good time, despite the somberness of the situation. All of the sudden, a frog—and I mean a huge frog—leapt onto my head. Startled, I screamed, and the frog jumped onto the next person's head, and so on and so on until the frog had jumped on every person (except my niece who ran) sitting around the table. Every one of us said, almost in unison, "That's Rob messing with us." Unbelievably, that same frog has been living in the same exact spot near that same table ever since that day. We all still call him Rob.

After some of the experiences that the skeptics can easily chalk up to coincidence (even I had a tendency to do so), there were a few experiences that finally satisfied my need to know that there is life after death. The first experience that could not be explained with logic came while I was talking to Rob's mother, Lorraine, one evening on the phone. We had talked quite a while, mostly about Rob. We reminisced, cried, and laughed a little. I cannot recall now the specifics of the conversation, but what happened during the conversation is forever burned into my mind. As we were talking, I walked inside from the back porch. When I opened the porch door and approached the kitchen, I could smell Lorraine's perfume. The smell was strong and distinct. There was no mistaking the smell, since she always wore it when she came to visit. Suffice to say, it is not my favorite smell. At first I did not fully interpret what had happened. When I did, I immediately told Lorraine.

I never told her I disliked the smell, but I guess the cat is out of the bag now. I stood in the kitchen for several minutes until the smell finally seemed to simply disappear. Lorraine and I agreed it had to be Rob somehow showing himself to us. After all, we had just been speaking of him.

The second event was witnessed not only by me but also by a friend, which made the experience that much more profound. My friend and I had gone to a football party in the neighborhood. I came home early, and my friend stayed. It had begun to rain softly, so I decided to lie on the porch couch and read my spiritual books. I had the radio on a soft rock station at a very low volume, barely audible, really. At some point, my friend showed up to check on me. I told him I was fine, and he came in for a bit. He joined me on the porch, and we began chatting. I told him about the book I was reading and some of the events that had occurred. Immediately, his skepticism kicked in, but the more we talked the more he seemed to recall instances that he felt Rob may have been trying to communicate with him. About that time, and completely without warning, the radio blasted so loudly that it distorted the speakers as if they were about to blow. I jumped off the couch and ran into the living room to turn it down. We were both stunned and speechless. I remember feeling excited and peaceful all at the same time.

Of course, it only took a moment for my friend to rationalize how this happened. He said without hesitation, "You must have sat on the remote. Where is it?" Well, it was at this point that he became witness to spiritual presence. The stereo receiver had been broken for many years. It had no working remote and the volume could only be adjusted by manually turning a dial. When I ran to turn it off, the dial was turned all the way up. It had to have been manually moved but we were the only people in the house and were nowhere even near the stereo. There simply is no other explanation. After this occurrence, I firmly believed in the spirit world. It brought me peace, but of course, I wanted more. Once again, I had forgotten my bartered promise to God to stop as soon as He allowed me to communicate with Rob.

A few nights after the stereo occurrence, I decided to further test my spirit communication skills. I wondered, if the previous events had happened when I was simply *thinking* about Rob and his existence as a spirit (a living soul), perhaps I could command his presence. I had finished reading the books that had gotten me to this point, and it was late. Initially, the plan was to turn in to bed and make the attempt the next day. Then an idea hit me. I had seen the lights flicker once before. If I could ask Rob to flicker the lights at my command, what more proof could I need? And so I did, and so he (or some soul) did.

Wanting even more, the next evening, I meditated again. I prayed for God's protection as the books had taught and then asked for Rob to come through. The truth is, I wanted to see him or hear him. I longed for something more tangible. I thought then I could be fully satisfied.

As I meditated and prayed, Rob's dog, Izabella, was lying next to me in the bed. Although I sensed nothing, no presence at all, Izabella jumped from the bed, ran to the window and began barking and growling. Growling is the key word here. I had never heard her growl and never have again since that moment. I tried to calm her, but she wouldn't stop and she wouldn't come back to bed. I became terribly frightened. All I could surmise is that I had a dark spiritual presence trying to come through. Surely, if it were Rob, Izabella would not be afraid. I prayed for protection, and I prayed for God to make it stop. Without knowing why, Izabella suddenly stopped barking and growling. She came back to bed seemingly unconcerned about what she had sensed. She lay down and went right off to sleep as if nothing had happened.

This time I kept my promise to God. There would be no more communicating with the spirit world, not intentionally, anyway. If it happened without my trying, that was fine, but I would not attempt it again. I would never invite spirits into my world again. Rob had let me know of his existence, and my wanting more was selfish and self-serving. I needed to let him go. Surely he had more important things to do now than answer my requests here on earth. A new and far more important journey for me was about to unfold.

WHY BAD THINGS HAPPEN TO GOOD PEOPLE

Once I halted my so-called spiritual journey, I had nothing to focus upon but work. Sure, that satisfied my mind during the day, but the nights were long and lonesome. My mother and friends warned me this would happen. I assured them that it wouldn't bother me since Rob often worked at night, so I was used to being alone at bedtime. As is always the case, my mother was right. I cried nightly, sometimes until I fell asleep.

Perhaps it was time to dissect why all of this had happened to Rob and me. If I now believed in the afterlife and again in God, then, what does it all mean? I focused on why God would take Rob away so tragically without even being able to say goodbye. After all, this was not how I had it planned. If he were to die it would be from cancer, and we would have time to plan and to say all the things we needed to say. That was the plan.

There had to be a purpose for his dying on the motorcycle in another state. Much to my surprise, it didn't take long for me to realize that the manner of Rob's death was exactly what he would have wanted and a blessing from God.

Remember he said, "…It will make for a nice wake, baby." It was as if Rob had some sense of knowing the end was near. More importantly, no matter how courageous he had been through the cancer battle, he shared with me that he was terrified of dying from it. He was terrified of becoming sicker and sicker and debilitated, and he feared the inevitable, irretractable pain. Most of all, he didn't want his family to watch him die.

Clearly, God had granted Rob a gift. Rob died instantly without suffering, without his family watching, and doing something he loved. In a strange sort of way, maybe the method was even a little easier on those left behind. I guess that could be debated depending on whom you asked. As I considered that perhaps God had blessed Rob by allowing him to go this way, how could I be angry with God for that? I couldn't. But why did He allow the suffering from cancer? I had to know.

As I pondered nightly about life and death I realized I had become a bit of a hermit focusing on nothing but work and the agony of my life and the questions that troubled my mind. This needed to change, and it was time. One evening shortly after that, I had some friends over. We enjoyed some wine together. It felt good to laugh a little.

At some point in the evening, I began to share some of the experiences I had had. Everyone supportively listened, and a few shared similar stories from their lives. As the night passed, I felt compelled to tell them what I had been obsessing over as of late. This was another enormous turning point in my journey with God, only I didn't know it yet. I shared with the group these words, "Everyone needs to know the answer to one question in life: Why do bad things happen to good people?" Certainly it was the question I was seeking to answer, and I explained that when I figured it out, I intended to write a book so that everyone in the world could have an understanding. That question created much debate among us. Many opinions swirled around. Most of us, even those in a close relationship with God, questioned the purpose of it all. The evening ended and of course, we had no definitive answer. As we closed the night down, we decided to attend church the next day and to go as a group.

The following morning, we arrived at church. Mind you, this was the first time I had been to church in many years and the first time since Rob's memorial. Nevertheless, given the kindness and generosity the church had showed me in my time of need, I wanted to go. Maybe this time it would be different. Maybe it would help me find the understanding I was seeking.

Attending church that morning was not only different than any previous church experience, it was literally, life-altering. As we walked into the sanctuary together, we retrieved our sermon bulletins. The bulletin had a large question mark on the front, and at the bottom was the name of the series: "Life's Biggest Questions." It seemed very ironic to me, but I didn't have much time to contemplate it as we hustled in to find a row of seats where we could all sit together. In the dimly lit sanctuary, we worshiped in song for a bit and then the pastor approached the stage. Just before he spoke, I opened the sermon bulletin. I couldn't believe what I was reading! My eyes welled up with tears, my heart raced and I felt like I was about to faint. With immense excitement in my voice, I whispered to the group to open their bulletins immediately. Everyone's eyes were instantly filled with tears but no one spoke. We just stared at each other, stunned and speechless. The sermon for the day was "Why Bad Things Happen to Good People?" After the service, we all agreed God had spoken directly to us. The words in the bulletin were exactly what we had discussed the night before. For that matter, the pastor's words were as well.

My mind raced with excitement as I thought, all that time I spent trying to talk to spirits, and God was trying to get me to talk to Him. Well, He had my attention now! This would not be the last time God spoke and I listened.

Of course, I almost couldn't wait to go to church the following Sunday. Surely I would get more, learn more. After a few weeks of the "Why bad things happen to good people" series, the following series was "What Happens When You Die." The one after that was "What's My Purpose?" How could the pastor have chosen the exact topics I needed so desperately? These were the exact three questions that had troubled my mind. My level of astonishment each week cannot be described. I didn't know why God had chosen me to converse with, but obviously He had. And I was listening. Finally, although I missed Rob terribly, I felt at peace. The pain of losing him eased some. My head was clearer. I knew he was with God, I knew I would see Rob again, and most of all, I knew there was some purpose for it all and for my life. Figuring it all out in detail would take some time, but what else did I have but time?

Many of the answers I sought are found in the book of Job, but not to worry; I won't be preaching any scripture here. I mention it so that you can explore on your own the lessons found in this part of the Bible. Besides, I am no biblical expert, only an expert on my own life. I'll leave the teaching to those who are properly equipped. As I write this book, trust that I am still just a student myself. My journey to God and with God will be eternal.

My approach to answering the "why bad things happen to good people" question started with simply thinking about the man Rob was. Those who knew him loved him. Those who met him even once admired him. Rob was patient and kind with everyone. He was always doing for others without any desire for recognition. People were drawn to him. Rob was talented and could do anything he set his mind to, and for that, he was admired by many. He was incredibly brave and courageous. He was an adoring and loving husband and a caring and patient father.

You get the idea? Rob fit the definition of "good people" easily, and there is no debate that bad things had happened to him.

Weeks passed, and my work continued. As I mentioned already, I worked out that God had allowed Rob to die in the manner Rob would have chosen. I was now thankful for that, and I decided to tell God so during my prayers. I worked out that when bad things happen to bad people, the death essentially goes unnoticed in the world. That is to say, if we perceive a person as bad—a murderer, for example—and that person dies, only his family and friends suffer. Therefore, only they have the opportunity to learn from the experience of suffering. Simply put, few lives will be positively changed at all.

Just a few days ago, I ran into a coworker of Rob's while I was shopping at Home Depot. After he asked how I was doing, he launched into a conversation about how Rob's death changed his thinking and his life. He discussed how healthy and strong Rob was until he got cancer and then how tragic it was that he died on the motorcycle. He knew of the many hobbies and associated "toys" Rob owned. You name it, Rob had it. He acknowledged what a strain it had been for me to take care of these after his death. The point he finally came to make was that he learned two very important lessons. The first is to plan ahead, and don't leave your loved ones overburdened with distributing things you accumulated. It's enough just to get through the grieving process. Second, and more importantly, he learned that we only have the moment we are in. We only have the second we breathe. Life can end without warning. I would guess that many who knew Rob learned these same life lessons.

As time has passed, I have spoken with several of Rob's closest friends. Each of them in some manner or another has parroted the concept that "life's too short." We all say this so frequently I believe it has nearly lost its meaning. How many times have you said it? Do you really live your life accordingly? Have you refocused on the things that really matter, or are you still consumed with the material things of the earthly world? I know that at least some of the people who loved and lost Rob have begun living a life centered on relationships and not on material goods. In the end, nothing matters except your relationships with your family, your friends and with God.

After moving to Jacksonville, Rob and I had built a big, beautiful home in an affluent neighborhood. We couldn't have been more proud. As time passed, and despite chemo treatments and such, we found time to make it our unique and special place. After all, Rob and I were not much for going out. We enjoyed our time together, and we enjoyed entertaining friends in our home. During the first round of chemo, Rob decided he wanted a pool. I desperately tried to talk him out of this because it would overextend us financially, at least beyond my comfort zone. He and a friend of ours, Leslie, used those old lines I just spoke of—"Life's too short" and "You only live once" —and somehow, I caved under their arguments. It was hard to say no in light of the cancer. Once the pool was in, we re-landscaped to make the backyard our haven. I planted an herb and vegetable garden every spring and secretly competed with the neighbors to see who could grow the most and best tomatoes.

After Rob died, I sat outside admiring the yard and pool, but it no longer brought me peace and happiness. It only brought me pain. All I could think as I sat there and cried was none of it meant anything without someone to share it with. I let my garden die because I realized that without Rob admiring my green-thumb talent, it didn't seem to matter. The garden may have just as well been a bunch of weeds. Eventually, I stopped going outside altogether because it only brought me pain.

As the weeks passed, I have no idea how many, I realized how terribly overwhelmed I was. How was I going to survive financially with this big house and big mortgage? Simply put, Rob and I, like so many, lived on a tight budget that required two incomes. My mind raced about how I would take care of the pool, which I knew nothing about, the house maintenance, and the yard work (which I used to love and now despised). Recall my mention of the importance of relationships? My family and Rob's family understood my dilemma. They knew that I should be focused only on grieving and not on how to pay the bills. Much to my surprise, my mother called one day and said, "Bob (Rob's father) has given you some money to help you get through." Bob and Nancy (Rob's stepmother, whom I believe is ultimately the final decision-maker) had granted me the most amazing gift. They gave me time to grieve. It was so generous that I was at a total loss for words for days. I didn't even know how to thank them because surely no words would measure up to the kindness and generosity they had shown.

Shortly thereafter, I recalled that my sister had given us money to help with the mortgage when I had lost my job. I had never used the money but had kept it in an account just in case. Between the two gifts, I had time to think, time to grieve, and time to make a plan. I am eternally grateful to them all. Needless to say, I forgot about the bills for several weeks and focused on the grief and my journey to understand it all.

Eventually, the time came to begin handling the financial matters that arise when someone dies, and I realized something that had totally escaped my mind until that moment. I seemed to recall that when I took my new job there was an option to cover my spouse with term life insurance. There was so much chaos during this time with Rob going through surgeries and chemo again that I honestly couldn't recall the details and wasn't absolutely sure that I had elected this option. I rummaged around my office until I found the paperwork. I was shocked to learn that I had in fact covered Rob, and it was for a fair amount. Not a lot, but certainly more than I expected, which was nothing. With Rob's life insurance, my policy on him, and the family gifts, I was able to refinance the house and get my head above water. This would be the first of many blessings I would receive.

While a part of me understood that this money would alleviate my financial worries, the more I thought about it, the sadder I felt. It was like a sense of guilt came over me although I couldn't understand why. I remember calling my mother and telling her that I didn't want the money. It felt like blood money to me in some weird way. I wanted Rob back, period. I would rather live in poverty with Rob than to have this stupid money. Of course, my mother's wisdom pulled me through to a clearer way of thinking simply by pointing out that if I had died before Rob, I had arranged to leave him a substantial amount of money so he would not have to worry. She explained that Rob would not want me to have to struggle and worry, and I could not argue her point. I can tell you, however—and this is the point I make about valuing your relationships—to this day, I would choose to live in poverty with Rob if given the chance. The money, the big house, the boats, cars, and such mean nothing. I cannot impress this upon you enough. Material things mean absolutely nothing without the love of your family.

Let's get back to that age-old question, "Why do bad things happen to good people?" When someone like Rob dies, it has the potential to positively change lives because the death profoundly touches and affects many people. Through biblical study, spiritual study, and considering my own beliefs, I learned that each of us has a purpose on earth. Once that purpose is fulfilled, our earthly life is over, and we are called home. That is, each of us possesses God-given talents. Yes, each of us. Some people go a lifetime without considering what their talent is and how it could be best used to serve others.

God-given talent doesn't mean you're an expert at something; it just means it comes naturally to you and it is enjoyable to you. Those who know me will agree whole-heartedly that my talent is language, preferably talking. Over the years, my family has told many stories at each family gathering about my early talking, early walking and, shall we say, assertiveness. I talked at eight months and walked at seven months. Of course, my vocabulary was lacking at such a young age, so I would become frustrated when an adult or my older sister didn't understand, which would induce, from what I have been told, one heck of a temper tantrum. I should have let my mother write this paragraph because she immensely enjoys telling these stories. Undoubtedly, I wasn't the easiest child to raise, but it makes for entertaining family humor today. The point is this: I have always loved talking. This natural God-given draw to language has also translated into my enjoyment of writing and hence, this book. Suffice to say, if I could stand on a platform and speak this book aloud where the entire world could hear, I would do so in a minute.

Now, I cannot say to this day exactly what Rob's talent was specifically. There were so many unique things about him. I do know this: Rob's kindness and compassion for people drove him to do many good deeds without recognition. He raised money for Relay of Life, he donated paint to the local high school art class, he helped rebuild a home for an employee who was financially desperate, and he gave his time to assist the disabled hunters. Simply put, he was always helping others. What I know for sure is that on July 17, 2010, Rob had used up his talents as God had planned for him to do, and he had fulfilled his earthly purpose. His fate in heaven was sealed, and he was gone from this earth and from all of those who loved him.

Given all the lessons I learned throughout my search for answers, I concluded that Rob's life and death was clearly meant to affect someone (or several people) in some positive way. His entire life had been spent positively helping and affecting others, so his death surely must have done the same. I thought that his death ironically had perhaps the most profound impact he ever made. I thought about it this way: When a famous artist, poet, or author dies, his works become much more valuable than when that person was alive. Well, Rob was no doubt famous in his own right, so his death must have had some positively significant influence upon people.

Everyone seemed to know and love Rob. As these ideas settled within in my mind, I recalled the memorial service where hundreds of people attended. There were so many, and I pondered if it was one of them who now found and understood their purpose as a result of Rob's death? Was someone dramatically changed by his death? In what way was that person changed? How would that person do good with what he or she had learned? I thought about a line in the memory card we chose for Rob's memorial and how fitting it was to my new understanding. It read in part, "...When you are lonely and sick of heart, go to the friends we know and bury your sorrows *in doing good deeds*. Miss me but let me go." Needless to say, as I wondered who would recognize their new purpose and what that purpose might be, I couldn't see the nose on my own face.

The sermon series continued, and I was drawn like a moth to a flame. I looked forward to Sundays. I adored and admired my pastor who had been with me from the beginning of this journey. I loved my church. I considered myself God's child now and had planned to be baptized. Surprisingly, I received an email from the church's pastor one day just before making that decision. It was the week before I was to be baptized. I read the email and wept. It took me quite a while to construct a reply, but eventually the words came. The pastor, Dave, asked if I would be willing to do a videotaped interview sharing "my story," as he called it. I didn't hesitate to correct him. My understanding at this point, you see, was that it was

Rob's story, not mine. He had suffered and died, not I. I later came to understand that the pastor was right. It is my story because I am the only one who can tell it. It is my story about Rob.

The pastor said he would like to incorporate the video into the sermon series for the congregation to view. He believed it would help people. At first, I thought there is no way I could talk about what had happened without crying and breaking down. It had only been a short time since Rob's death. The emotions were still so raw. Then, I wondered how my painful story would help anyone. Wouldn't it just make people sad? I didn't want people to pity me. Eventually, I agreed to do it based solely upon my trust that Pastor Dave knew what he was doing.

Before the taping, Dave prayed with me. It gave me chills. I remember thinking, I wish I could pray that eloquently. He then took a few minutes to explain how the taping would be done and once again the purpose behind it. Although I couldn't see my own strength at this point, he did. He assured me that I would do great and that we could re-tape as many times as we needed. At that moment, I had forgotten that my God-given talent is talking. The pastor explained that the goal was to share with people the terrible tragedy of Rob's illness and death and how it brought me to Christ. He also explained that I needed to sum it up in about one minute. "That's not possible," I thought but did not say. Following his explanation, however, it made sense why he wanted me to tell this sad story of mine, and I felt honored to have the chance to reach others. Maybe my pain could bring someone else to Christ. Maybe this was my purpose.

The videographer started recording and I took a deep breath and began talking. I did the interview and never cried once. I came close, but held it together and got through it. When I stopped talking I immediately realized that I had no idea what I had said. It was like God was holding my hand, saying, "You can do it," and he filled my mouth with words. I asked Dave how it went and admitted I couldn't recall a single word I had said. It was a blur, a fog, almost like I wasn't even present. I asked if I said, "um" too often, which I know is a bad habit of mine when I am nervous and which is not a good trait when practicing law. Usually, I am acutely aware of it, but I couldn't seem to remember anything I said. Pastor Dave assured me I didn't say "um" even once and that I had done great. He proclaimed it was exactly what he had hoped for. I was shocked that we didn't have to do another taping but was hugely relieved. And then came the words I never wanted to hear. Pastor Dave said, "I hope you know you're going to be a celebrity in the church after this is shown." I blushed and explained I wasn't looking forward to that at all.

The following Sunday, the video was shown at the end of the sermon. It was the day of my baptism so my family and friends were there to see it. I felt like I was seeing it for the first time, too, since I couldn't remember any part of it. I was proud that I had done it and Dave was right: People I had never spoken to before approached me and thanked me. Several talked about how it helped them to remember to keep life in perspective. I received cards from some acknowledging the video and offering their assistance to me should I need anything. If nothing else, I learned that pain bonds us to each other and to God. I felt like my family had just grown a hundred fold. I now had a church family.

I continued working on my new relationship with God and pursuing the answer to why bad things had happened to Rob. Truthfully, not everything I learned from scripture made sense as I applied it to Rob. All the suffering he endured hadn't improved his relationship with Christ. He rarely attended Church, and I had come to think he no longer prayed. I knew I hadn't prayed much over the course of things, so I doubted he had. I worried about that. One day that I actually cannot specifically recall now, I had that "aha" moment.

It hit me! How could I have missed this? The lesson was never about Rob. It was about me. In trying to figure this whole life purpose thing out, I had spent my months thinking only about Rob and his purpose. Why had Rob suffered was my focus, never acknowledging that I had suffered along with him every step of the way. Maybe Rob didn't need to improve his relationship with Christ, as I had believed. He was always doing good deeds and lived his life in a Christian manner. Maybe he had prayed and just not with me. He even seemed to know exactly when he was going home to God. It became so clear that this entire time God had been trying to reach me. He had tested my faith over and over. He gave me chance after chance to come to Him, and I had either given up or flatly refused. As this all rushed into my mind like a tornado, I still found it hard to shift the focus to myself. Doing so felt wrong, somehow, like I was disrespecting Rob in some way. I felt guilty thinking about myself instead of Rob, so I prayed about it.

This epiphany changed everything. Now, I had to start all over again in my thinking. I prayed for the answers. It was about this time that I learned the importance of journaling. I had so much information and so many experiences in my head that I feared some would get lost along the way. I began writing every relevant thought down. Once I began journaling something inside me changed. I couldn't stop thinking about my purpose in life and how that was tied to all of these painful experiences. As I used my God-given language talent by journaling, things suddenly became much clearer. There was something about seeing it on paper. It didn't make sense just yet, but I was changed.

One afternoon I watched a talk show about a woman who had survived the most horrific and unimaginable domestic abuse at the hand of he husband. In short, after beating his wife, he set her on fire. She lived but was forever physically scarred and disfigured from the burns. I watched this woman tell her story, and I was amazed by her strength. I thought to myself, I couldn't have endured that. It was at that moment I realized what I believe is my calling, my purpose. I knew I had to tell my story. I had to write a book to share it with the world in a way that would help people heal through the pain of losing a loved one. I had to write it in such a way that it would bring those who don't know Christ to Him. For those who already know Him, I had to convey the importance of never losing faith in the face of pain, challenges, tragedy, and heartache.

From that day forward, I thought about the book daily. I told my mother time and again that I honestly felt compelled by God to do this. I had no idea where to start, but I was certain somehow I would figure it out. I thought about writing the book constantly but never seemed to find the time between work and completing my master's program. The compulsion to write this book ate at me almost to the point of obsession. I talked about it to friends and family far too often. I knew if I didn't write it soon instead of simply talking about doing it, eventually, no one would want to listen to my dreams of grandeur.

One afternoon I was in the grocery store when the words "passionate pursuit" seemingly popped into my head out of nowhere. I recall thinking, "that might just be a good name for a book." I didn't have my journal or a piece of paper even so I jotted these words into the notepad feature on my cell phone. I didn't think about it again because frankly I forgot.

The following Sunday, April 17, 2011, the sermon series "One Week to Live" began. As usual, everything I heard was eye opening. I listened intently. I asked myself, "What would my life look like if I knew I only had a week to live? What in life have I chased the most? Did I accomplish anything that matters?" As I pondered and listened, the pastor said, "Jesus passionately pursued God's will. Have that same *passionate pursuit* for your own life and for God's Glory." I couldn't believe what I had heard! There were *my* words in the sermon again. I had written these very words down a week before and stored them in my cell phone. In my excitement, I reached into my purse and pulled out my cell phone. I opened the notepad that contained the words, tapped a friend on the knee, and said, "Look at this." I guess I needed someone else to feel God's presence in a real way. He hadn't been to church in a while, so I thought this would deepen his belief and pull him back towards Christ. Thus, I was already starting to fulfill my life purpose at that very moment. I was bringing others to faith.

Well, there it was again. God had spoken to me. This time, however, I felt I knew the full meaning behind his message; it was loud and clear. There was nothing to ponder or study when I returned home. Nope. I knew exactly what God was saying, and it was, "Julie, write the book, and do it now." As the weeks passed I could find words in each sermon that reassured me to write a book that would help others. You might be surprised that I never told my pastor of these "conversations" that God had shared with me via his sermons. Pastor Dave was totally unaware how God was using him in this very specific way. Well, Dave, now you know.

Let's go back to the first time Dave and I met. It was to discuss what would be said at Rob's memorial service. One of the first things Dave said to me and Rob's family that day was, "You are not here by accident. I don't believe in accidents." That was a painful day. I imagine he elaborated, but I just don't remember the rest of what he said. But I cannot forget those words. Whatever the case, how true those words were and how clear they had become to me now.

At this point, you know much about Rob, God, and me. What I haven't shared is the day of Rob's memorial—the day that was supposed to be his "celebration of life" party. Pastor Dave spoke first. He delivered a message so touching that it sounded as if he had known Rob for many years. Kindness like that which I saw in Rob exuded from Dave, and it made my heart happy.

When it was time for me to speak and deliver Rob's eulogy, I stepped upon the stage and was uncontrollably shaking. Most people thought it was fear of speaking to a large group. That was not it at all. That has never bothered me. My fear was whether I would remember the words without looking at the paper so that Rob would be proud that I was speaking from my heart. Also, I feared horribly that I would simply not be able to speak at all. I was afraid my emotions would take over, and I would leave the stage a crying and weak mess. Again, my fear was of letting Rob down. I had made him this promise, and I had to fulfill it. It was the last thing I could do for Rob, and it had to be perfect. As I walked to Dave to retrieve the microphone, I told him, "You're going to have to hold me up and hold this paper because I can't read it for all the shaking." We both giggled a bit. Dave put his arm around me, pulled me to his side, and held the paper as I began to speak. I got through that horrific moment and without realizing it began my new life.

When You Fail, Don't Blame God.

Go to Him!

As I was nearing the end of writing this book, I realized, the hard way, how spiritually lost I had become all over again. Moreover, I wasn't even aware that, in some ways, I had returned to some old habits I had previously repented over. I had lost my immense focus on God and seemed to think constantly about Rob's death and how unfair life had been and continued to be. My beliefs about God hadn't changed, mind you. I had just lost focus. Depression was taking over again, although I wasn't sure why. This made no sense. I asked myself why was I struggling more a year after his death than I had in the past. I knew Rob was with God. I knew what my purpose in life was, and I was passionately pursuing it. I had answered the questions I needed to answer. I had even begun dating and felt a sense of moving onward. Why, then, had pain crept into my soul once again, and why did it seem to worsen by the day?

I cried often and decided at times to numb my pain with wine. Jesus drank wine, right? This was obviously a lousy excuse but the best one I could muster. Understand that I am not proud of this behavior, but pride has no place in this book, only honesty. If you are suffering the loss of a loved one you will no doubt identify with my behavior, but rest assured numbing the brain is not the answer. Nevertheless, the pain didn't lessen, and the more I hurt, the more I wallowed in it until I had effectively destroyed at least one relationship and was straining a couple more. Those in my life neither knew what to say or do, nor understood why I had become this way, seemingly out of the blue. Frankly, I didn't understand it either. But the pain was real, and I couldn't seem to deal with it. I prayed but not nearly as often as I should have. Yes, after all I have previously written, I, too, fell very short of remembering that it is God's agenda, and He would see me through it. I just wallowed in my sorrow and became more and more isolated.

What I hadn't realized was that the month of July had crept up on me, and it was nearing the one-year anniversary of Rob's death. Finally, when the grief became so intense that I felt I could no longer cope, I sought the help of a counselor, something I had been too proud to do previously. Thankfully, she explained the natural phenomenon that happens during the month of a loved one's death. Essentially, most everyone has a very difficult time during this period. It usually continues for many years—perhaps forever—but eventually to a lesser degree. This gave me some peace, for at least I had some rationale for why I felt so down. It was no excuse, however, for not turning to God, each and every day, to get me through it. Nothing good would be found in the bottom of that wine glass or from hiding under my bed sheets. Nevertheless, I prayed occasionally, went to counseling every week, and hoped it would just pass.

If you recall from the "Passionate Pursuit" chapter, where I tell of having my "aha" moment (realizing that all the pain and suffering was to bring me to God), then you may know where this is going. God can and will refocus you when you fall off course. For those who don't pay attention, expect to continue down a path that will be emotionally and spiritually void. Nevertheless, despite all I had learned and come to believe, I was certainly off course so let me share with you how He refocused me.

God simply added to the pain I was already experiencing. That is, on the very day of Rob's death, one year later, God shook me to my very core. A few days before July 17 I decided I had to get away. I felt the need to get out of the house Rob and I had shared and leave those memories behind for a bit. On a last-minute whim, I packed up my two Shelties, Izabella and Spencer, and headed to the beach at Amelia Island Plantation. This is one of the most beautiful places I've seen, and it is only two hours away. I thought I could unwind there and say a sort of "goodbye" to Rob on the beach. We were married on the beach, so this seemed like the perfect place to meditate, pray, and say goodbye. It had been a year, but somehow I felt like I had to "let him go." I was tired of hurting, and this seemed like the only answer. I also thought it would be an inspiring place to bring this book to completion. We were to stay a week, but it appeared I had packed for a month, dragging along with me my book work, computers, and dog supplies. Unfortunately, due to God's little "wake-up call," we stayed only two-and-a-half days.

I checked in with the dogs on Sunday, the anniversary day I had so dreaded. That evening, I took the dogs to the beach. We all played in the water and I drew a goodbye note to Rob in the sand. The dogs enjoyed the outing tremendously, playing with each other and every kid they came across as we walked for miles down the beach. When I returned to the room, I felt a peace I hadn't in a long time. I grabbed my computer and worked on the book while the dogs napped.

The next day was much the same. We played on the beach in the morning, afternoon, and evening, and I worked on the book in the time between. That evening, I felt so peaceful and slept well. Looking back now, at this point, I cannot remember the last time I had thanked God for all the blessings he had given me or the strength He was obviously providing me at that moment. How could I not have seen how many wonderful things I had in my life as I admired God's beautiful world? Nevertheless, as many of us do, I had slipped into my old way of thinking and had begun taking things for granted.

The next evening I took the dogs outside the room and sat upon a grassy hill overlooking the beach. I took in the beauty and wonder of the earth. I listened to the ocean roar and felt the wind in my hair. I took pictures of the dogs lounging in the grass, clearly content and relaxed. At some point my mind wandered back into the book. There was a detail that I couldn't recall that I wanted included in the book. I knew one of Rob's friends could remind me, so I gave her a call. We talked for a bit, reminisced about Rob, and she retold the story I was wondering about. I shed a few tears as she sweetly reassured me of my inner strength. As we chatted away, I failed to notice that Izabella had wondered away from me, something extremely unusual for her. When I did notice, I began calling for her. She did not come. Again, this was an unusual behavior for her. After a few minutes, panic set in.

Izabella, Rob's therapy dog through the illness and suffering, had seemingly vanished into thin air. She was beside me one minute and gone the next. In state of panic I reminded myself that she was well trained and had proved very trustworthy over the years of traveling to the mountains and beaches. I tried to convince myself that she was nearby and simply couldn't hear me over the roar of the ocean, and I couldn't see her in the dark of night. As I frantically searched, two kids joined me with flashlights. We walked the beach back and forth, thinking she had gone there because of her love for the water. There was no sight of her.

Hours had passed. I knew I needed much more help than just the two children, but I wasn't thinking clearly and wasn't sure whom to call besides hotel security. I came back to the room to check on Spencer and an angel appeared. A woman I had never met came down to my room in her pajamas and asked how she could help. It was her children who had been searching late into the night. She convinced me to sit down and think about how to handle getting Izabella back.

As we discussed Izabella's disappearance and tried to determine the best action plan, she asked where my husband was and whether he was helping me search. Of course, the floodgates opened. I was right back to wallowing in self-pity, but now I had someone new who would listen and feel sorry for me.

After hearing my pathetic tale about why I had come there and why my husband was not helping, my angel launched into gear and got a full search team in place. She called the local police and convinced them to join the search. She had hotel security working in tandem with the local police. As my mind cleared, I called friends and Sheltie Rescue to get help searching in the morning and they notified animal control and the Humane Society.

In less than an hour, a police officer came to my hotel door. He spoke with hotel security that had spotted Izabella, and off we went in his patrol car to continue the search. My angel and her daughter offered to stay in my hotel room with Spencer, who was quite stressed at this point. She said they would wait for my return. The officer and I searched for Izabella until 4:30 in the morning, at which point my body simply gave out. I had to lie down. Not only had I lost the little dog

I loved so dearly, but worst of all I had lost Rob's dog, Izzy, just two days after the anniversary of his death. How could I have let this happen? I ran through it in my mind over and over and blamed myself for trusting her too much. The thought of never finding her consumed me. I cried myself to sleep.

I woke up that morning at 7:30, which is Izabella's time for breakfast. I thought if she had been holed up for the night, she would be on the move around this time. Sheltie Rescue was on the way, friends were on the way, and the hotel security and the local police had turned the case over to the next shift. I walked and I prayed, and I prayed, and I prayed, and I begged God to return her to me. I would repent later for having lost my focus.

As if He heard my request, within an hour, hotel security notified me they were in pursuit of Izabella. She, of course, was completely terrified and in flight mode at this point, so she would come to no one. A valet worker immediately picked me up to take me to her. The driver sped through the narrow streets talking on his radio to the security officer until we met up. He told me that she was coming across the golf course and to jump out of the van. I did, even before the van had fully stopped. I ran over a hill and onto the golf course, and there she was! I saw her little face and her little eyes, and they were filled with fear. She was muddy from head to toe. She was about fifty feet away from me, but I could tell she was going to run if I wasn't careful. I sat down in the grass and began using all the vocabulary words she knows (which, by the way, are quite a few). I kept talking to her for what seemed like an eternity but was probably less than a minute, until finally, her face changed. She recognized me, and here she came! She ran toward me and leapt into my arms almost knocking me over. I cried and thanked God while she licked my face all the way to the hotel room to show her sincere appreciation. We all slept the rest of the afternoon from pure exhaustion.

When I woke up that evening, I took the dogs for a walk on the beach as usual but something was wrong. I didn't feel right, and as I continued to walk, I realized what was wrong. Having been through this quite embarrassing illness five years prior, I knew that getting to the emergency room as quick as possible was critical. I packed as fast as I could, loaded up the dogs, and headed for home.

On the two-hour drive home I couldn't even believe it all. My planned one-week beach retreat to deal with Rob's death, finish my book, meditate, and pray had turned into a total disaster. I barely had time to think of Rob. Now, I would be facing a round of surgeries and this time I would face them alone, without Rob. The closest family I have is two hours away. I dwelled on the fact that I had gone away to feel better, and at the moment, I felt worse than I had in many months. I had already been slipping, and here I was again saying, "Why me, God?" I hated the idea but knew I was falling victim to self-pity again and feared it would stick around for a while. I had gone away to rid myself of it yet I was returning home worse. "Unimaginable" was all I could think.

After the emergency room visit I was on bed rest for several days. I was in pain and bored to tears at the same time. The first day that I was able to get out of bed I realized my pool pump had burned out, which would cost around $400. I also realized my grass in the backyard died while I was gone due to invasion of armyworms. All I could think was what next? What else could possibly go wrong in just one week? I couldn't believe all that had happened or fathom why it had to be *this* particular week. The depression that had been stalking me that entire month was back and with a vengeance. I hated my life, and I cried day after day almost nonstop. The only thing I did right was thank God every day for returning Izabella to me. Each time I looked at her little face I thought about how it would've felt to never see her again and not know what happened to her. I was sure God had his hand on her return, but I could not understand why the trials would not end.

After about a week, it hit me! What was I doing? I turned into my old self, full of self-doubt, and hopelessness. I dove into the Bible, read previous sermon notes, and I watched recorded episodes of Joel Osteen. I read biblically based books about loving your life. I even reread what I had written in this book thus far. I prayed so hard every day that I found it difficult to come up with something unique to say to God each time. I prayed until it all made sense and then knew I would never stop praying again. Ever!

So, there is an answer to the "why me" in all this. God had brought me so far, until July hit when I lost track. I lost focus. I stopped putting Him first. He had to show me the way back. Knowing I'm no easy nut to crack, perhaps a little too strong for my own good, He had to make it good, so good that I couldn't help but pay attention! Looking back, God's love for me is the reason that He threw these challenges into my life, one right after another for days on end. He had to make it so hard that I would realize again that I can't go it alone and would run back into His graces. My knees spent quite a bit of time on the hard wood floors beside my bed those next few days. I even joked with myself at one point that I should buy myself some kneepads. Sometimes I prayed at the dock at the lake, as it seemed to add a certain serenity. The point is, I prayed, and I prayed hard. As I continued reviving my devotion to God, I recalled the quote by Rick Warren, "You'll never know God is all you need until God is all you got." Believe me, after the week I had, God was all I had. This nut was cracked! Lesson learned, and this time for good.

IMPERFECT PEOPLE

The experiences I have described that solidly affirmed my devotion to God come with a caveat. This is another quote I learned from Pastor Dave Willis that I think is absolutely essential for every Christian's understanding of life. "We are imperfect people loving a perfect God." I say this to you because we will all falter. I will and you will. We will all sin from time to time, and some more than others. Only Jesus was without sin and imperfection. In fact, throughout the Bible, you will read that God used imperfect and flawed people for His glory. What I know now, and I hope you either have come to know or will seek out for yourself, is that God loves us despite our imperfections. God wants a relationship with us, period. In having that relationship, expect your faith to be tested, but never lose it. That has been my personal struggle during all the difficult times. It still is today to be honest. I think many people going through great pain or crisis struggle with their faith as well. Don't! Struggle with the circumstances, not your faith, and know that God is with you and that He will see you through it. God gave each of us the required strength to deal with the challenges that come before us. That strength is already in you. Know that your struggle is for some purpose that you cannot understand at the moment but that through this struggle God is preparing you for something great in your future. Always believe He has a purpose for you. Believe and thank God in advance for those things that you desire to come to pass.

If you are reading this after having lost a loved one, please learn from my mistakes. For that matter, whatever the reason you are reading this, remember what you have learned by reading about my journey. Since we all know that death is a part of life, you, too, will one day go through the pain. It's inevitable. Hopefully, you will be better spiritually prepared than I was.

My story is told to you bluntly and truthfully. I have divulged to you how many times I lost my faith in God and even questioned His existence altogether. Trust me; I am not proud of it. You will likely be tempted to do the same during difficult times in your life. We are constantly being tempted by this earthly world, even when you are not involved in a God-given struggle and things appear perfect. If you don't attend a Bible-based church, I encourage you to find one. It might take a few tries until you find the right fit, but keep searching. It will come. If you don't have a relationship with Christ, begin building one.

I firmly believe that my pastor and my church, which I was drawn to by God's will and not by accident, saved my life. Had Dave not been the man he is and opened his heart, soul and church to me when I needed it most, I doubt I would have ever reached this level of spiritual growth. The experiences that followed meeting Dave were as close to talking directly to God as most will ever know. It still amazes me when I think back upon it. Seek out God, and He will be there with open arms. He wants a relationship with you, and trust me: you need a relationship with Him.

LESSONS LEARNED

During this journey of mine to understand life, death, and my purpose in this world, I learned many practical things that I continue to use in my life on a daily basis. Today, these ideas seem more like common sense, but in the middle of the grief, I could not see them at all. I hope you find these "tips" helpful, comforting, and applicable to your experiences.

It has been just over one year after Rob's death as I am finalizing the writing of this book. I have hurt much and have hurt hard; it my life's purpose to make it just a little easier for others. Nothing will make it painless, and you will still have to get through the process, but I sincerely hope my story will help you heal more easily than I did. More importantly, I hope that my personal experience and conversations with God will bolster your belief in Him and strengthen you immeasurably. These are my "pay it forward" thoughts and tips about grieving.

How to Grieve Properly

There is no proper way. There is no right way or wrong way. Don't let anyone tell you there is. There is only *your* way. That's not to say that many books and theories haven't been written. They have. I've read many of them. Some helped a little, but mostly because I realized other people in similar situations felt the same as I did, at least at times. Quite simply, just knowing others went through it and survived was comforting, but I found little else helpful in the books on *how* to grieve. All I can assure you is that you will have to go through it, and it will not be easy. Do it your way; don't let others apply rules to your grief; retreat from those who do not provide encouragement and peace; most of all, hold on to God, and you *will* come out on the other side stronger and perhaps even incredibly enlightened.

Grieve Like You Live

Remember this! I believe you will grieve in much the same way as you handle other crises in life. I also believe there is no time frame to follow; there are no set of feelings you should expect and certainly no order in which to expect them. As I said before, there is no right way or wrong way to grieve. You may be like I was and want to read every book you can find to validate your feelings. Go ahead! You may choose to avoid things like home movies of your loved one. Fine! Do whatever helps you. Just know that you will feel what you feel when you feel it. Each person's story of loss is unique, and therefore your grief process will be unique. Do not try to fit your grief into some mold or theory. It's yours and God's, and you two alone own it. Most important, if you attempt to squeeze your grief into some model, you will likely miss the most important part of the experience. You may miss the only pleasant part of it all, finding YOUR purpose.

Let Go of the Guilt

It is almost inevitable that you will experience guilt about something during the grief process. I felt guilty about having an argument with Rob before he died, for moving the photos that reminded me of him, for taking off my wedding rings, and for dating. That's just to name a few of the things I felt guilty about. Guilt crept in quite often during my grieving until I learned to let it go. Guilt has no place in Heaven where there is only love, so it should have no place here on earth. It is a useless emotion because it is only relevant to the past, which you cannot change. The one you lost who resides in Heaven harbors no guilt and does not want you to feel guilt. Guilt will do nothing but delay your healing. Apologize to the one you loved, confess it to God and repent if you believe you should, but whatever you do, let it go.

Don't Doubt Your Faith in God.

Or, if You Haven't Found Faith Yet, Find It Now!

Simply put, God will provide your life with struggles and challenges. It is not meant to hurt you, even though it will. Pain is meant to stretch you, equip you, and teach you, and most of all for God to reach you. Consider this: When you're at the gym and your personal trainer says, "No pain, no gain," what do you think he means? You can't grow larger muscles unless you literally push it to the limit, which causes injury to the muscle. God will push us to the limit at times. He will injure us at times. Keep faith that the resulting growth will be used for something great in your life. You may not understand it for some time, and maybe never, but staying steadfast during the hardest of times will be rewarded both on earth and in heaven.

Forgive

Depending on the events of your loved one's death, this may or may not apply, but it does apply to life in general. For your own sake, forgive the person who passed for whatever he or she had done in the past. Forgive the person for leaving you. Holding on to anger and resentment only adds to your pain. Only you suffer from not forgiving. Remember, your loved one is in Heaven where only love is known. You may also need to forgive those who hurt you along the way of your grieving process. Remember, I told you I could write a book of all the dumb things people say when someone dies. Mostly, their intentions are good, and they have no idea the pain they are inflicting. Forgive them. Chances are you will say something dumb when you are faced with consoling someone else one day. Trust me; I did, and I almost couldn't believe it. I felt like such an idiot. I, of all people, should have known what to say. I didn't, and out came something stupid.

Acknowledge That Your Loss and Grief Is Forever

Through my personal journey with grief and talking with others who have lost husbands long before I did, I've learned that grief is forever. It doesn't sound very uplifting, and for that I'm sorry. But you may as well know the truth. What you should also know, however, is that grief becomes less and less acute, and it need not consume you or your life. You will learn to manage it and move onward. You will be happy again. It will not be part of your everyday life forever. When the memories sneak in, you will still feel pain, but you will also feel happiness in remembering the person you loved. Think of it this way: Pain is temporary; misery is optional. Don't choose misery.

On that note, make sure those closest in your life understand this. Recall that I told you I had begun dating? My very first "non-negotiable" was, and still is, that anyone I date must understand I will always love Rob, he will always be my husband (I did not divorce him), and that I will always grieve his death, on some level. I am so very fortunate to have a wonderful man in my life today who fully understands this and I doubt he will ever realize my appreciation for that.

You see, I still can't even tell a happy story about Rob without at least a little tear (sometimes a full-on cry). Sometimes I see or hear something that brings back memories and I well up with tears. Others need to understand that the tears and heartache may last, but they are managed and eventually will no longer interfere with your life.

Nurture Your Relationships

Hopefully, you will find this to be an easy task and even an obvious one. Rob and I had the gift of cancer to teach us this. We had four years to think about what matters in life. Cancer taught us to create dreams and gave us the perseverance to fulfill them while we were still together. After losing Rob, I also learned that when your time comes to leave this earth, the only things that will matter are your relationships with God, your family, and your friends. You will not care what job title you attained, how much money you have, or how big your house is. If you don't believe me, think about it. Consider you are told you have one week to live. What would matter to you? Remember what I shared with you. After Rob died and I realized I had enough money to get my financial affairs in order, but I didn't even want the money. Honestly, I didn't. I hated the money. Don't get me wrong, I was grateful – but I didn't want it or the house because it all seemed to mean nothing without Rob to share it with me. All I wanted was my husband back. Nothing else mattered. Please don't wait until it's too late to strengthen your relationships. I'm still working on a few of mine, so I understand sometimes it can be quite difficult. Nevertheless, do it now, and do it consistently.

Avoid Toxic People

When Rob first died, people poured out love and support for me that was frankly amazing. I felt so blessed to have such a wonderful support system. Be aware, however, that even those who intend to support you may become toxic to you. Especially, in the early and most painful stages of your grief, avoid people who think their feelings are more important than yours. Their feelings are not, period! If they cannot understand this, retreat. This may sound harsh but I am certain it is good advice. Eventually you will be able to put others first but only you can decide when that time is. Avoid people who won't let you talk about your loss. Talking about it is part of healing. Most importantly, whenever possible, avoid anyone or any situation that will bring you more pain. Your grief is more than enough to handle. Forgive these people, but rid yourself of them and do it immediately. Once you are healed, you may decide the relationship is worth saving, but until then avoid it.

Don't Let Grief Define You

This may be your toughest challenge, especially in the beginning. For those who lose a spouse, it seems that all of a sudden, you are no longer someone's husband or wife; you are a widowed person. Frankly, I despise that word. You can become consumed with the pain of your loss to the point that it becomes your identity. I know because I allowed it to happen to me before I began my search for God. Everywhere you go in the beginning, people are saying how sorry they are for your loss. Cards will flood in saying the same things. You may feel like "you" disappeared, and this widowed person appeared in your place. I cannot tell you the best way for you to handle this, since we are all unique, and our losses are unique. But I can tell you what I did. I never stopped referring to myself as Rob's wife. I did not divorce Rob, and Rob still exists (although not on an earthly plane); ergo, we are still married. I will always be Rob's wife. Rob's mother will always be my mother-in-law and his father will always be my father-in-law. Should I ever remarry, well, then, I will have (in my heart) two husbands and one heck of an extended family. Why not? My point in this paragraph is this: Do whatever you must so that the death and the grief do not become *who* you are and they don't somehow define you.

This tip cannot be summed up with one or two examples. Take it for what it says, and remember it each time you are faced with a decision. I mention this because the same people who view you as the victim widow or widower will also see you as vulnerable. No matter how smart you are or how successful you've been in your life, someone will warn you that during this time of grief you are not capable of making good decisions. Believe me, there will be many decisions that must be made following the death of a loved one, and dealing with them will not be easy. Maybe you will feel vulnerable; maybe you won't. If you do, seek help from those you trust. Regardless of how strong you are, your heart is broken, and you are not emotionally *your* normal. Think about choices carefully. Run your thoughts past someone you trust, such as a close family member. I believe if you can lead with you brain and not with your heart, you will make solid choices, but I also believe that is easier said than done. Please be cautious and careful as you navigate through all the decisions.

Be Prepared to Explain What Happened to Your Loved One

This is probably easiest to explain by way of a story.

Eight months after Rob's death, one seemingly normal Saturday afternoon, I decided to take Rob's truck for a drive. It had been sitting in the driveway for weeks and needed to be driven. I went to the pool supply store, and the owner, whom I had only met once several years prior, asked me how Rob was doing. Apparently, he knew Rob had been battling cancer, and he was concerned since he hadn't seen him in the store for a long while. I explained what had happened the best I could with tears in my eyes and a shaking voice and then practically ran from the store.

Then, if that wasn't bad enough, immediately after, I stopped at the convenience store, began filling up the truck with gas and went inside to get a cold drink. When I approached the counter to pay, the convenience store clerked asked me how Rob was doing. There it was again! Before I spoke, I angrily thought, "When people would stop asking me this?" I hated having to say Rob was gone and then answer questions about what happened. Nothing ever sounded right. I tried Rob is dead. Rob was killed. Rob died in a wreck. Rob passed away. It didn't matter how I said it, the pain would rush back, and the person asking would expect an explanation. Finally, and before answering his question, I asked the clerk, whom I had never seen before, "How do you know I belong to Rob?" not even realizing I was driving Rob's truck, which he had recognized. Greif can make your brain a little fuzzy like that.

Eventually, I told the clerk what had happened, and his eyes welled with tears, as he said, "I'm so sorry. Rob was such a nice guy." As I drove home I thought, "Only Rob would take the time to befriend the local convenience store clerk." I smiled in admiration of my husband. I was lucky to have had him.

With that said, I certainly cannot tell you the best way to prepare yourself when this happens, but I can tell you that it will happen and usually when you least expect it. I think if I had known this in advance, the painful blow would have been a little less. Be prepared and maybe it won't be so difficult for you.

Embrace Doing Things
That Will Make You Question Your Own Sanity

Again, this is probably best explained by sharing with you some of the odd things I did, particularly during the early stages of my grief. Immediately after Rob's memorial, I had this horrific feeling of loss, abandonment, and loneliness. It was so overwhelming that I looked for ways to lessen the pain and to somehow feel close to him. Night after night I slept with the clothes he had died in. They smelled like motorcycle exhaust, but it didn't matter. Night after night I slept with his urn. I refused to wash my sheets until his scent had faded away. Insane? Perhaps a little, but at that moment if felt completely normal. I share this with you so you will expect such things. If you know someone who is grieving and his or her actions seem plain crazy at times, they're not! Don't judge yourself or anyone who does seemingly odd things during the grief process. It's OK to act weird. Embrace it. Eventually, you will put that urn on the mantle.

Eventually, you will wash those sheets. Eventually, you will move that pair of shoes that were left in the middle of the floor (oh, yes, a pet peeve that became something I adored after Rob was gone). It will all happen, eventually.

Time Alone Does Not Heal Your Wounds

Remember I mentioned all the stupid clichés people say during your grief? "Time heals all wounds" is one I learned to despise, and I heard it over and over and over again. I will admit there is some level of truth buried within the words, but time alone is not enough. It does make the pain a little easier to handle, but it does not make it miraculously go away. Here is what I do firmly believe about time healing wounds. It is not the passing of time alone that heals; it is what you decide to do during that time. Consider the story I told early on about the husband and wife whose son was killed by a drunk driver. The father never healed. Time alone never fixed his heartache. Time only resulted in his broken marriage and ultimately his own death. The mother went on to do great things in memory of her son. If you sit back waiting for the day that all of a sudden you feel better because two years have passed, you will never heal. You must take an active role and do something that matters with the time. I began a journey to understand life's purpose, my purpose, and to build an unshakable relationship with God. I began a journey to help others heal from their loss. I began this book.

Consider a Grief Group or Grief Counseling

In the area where I live I was not fortunate enough to have a grief group for younger widows and widowers. The only options were independent counseling, hospice groups, and funeral homes that offered counseling. What I learned by reaching out for help was incredibly unfortunate. I attended one group session and only one. When a woman who appeared to be in her seventies or so said to me, "How dare you compare your grief to mine. I was married to my husband for fifty years. You can't begin to relate to my feelings. You were only married for five." I was shocked! Because I was raised with southern manners, I chose not to respond rather than fire back with what I was thinking, which was, "How dare you say that to me? You were so lucky to have your husband so long. I only got five years with mine, and most of those years were filled with disease, heartache, and pain."

The point I make here is this: While these groups mean well, be cautious. You could end up feeling worse because you don't fit in. At thirty-nine years old, my grief was simply different from that of someone much older than I. I still had to go to work, function in life, and consider making a new life altogether. Many who are widowed young have children to care for as a single parent. The dynamics are endless. Find a group or counselor that suits you and your loss. If you don't have a group in your area, consider my answer to the dilemma. Start your own!

When in Doubt, Seek God Out

I have said this in many different ways throughout this book but I think it is well worth repeating and it is a great way to bring this book to its end. Remember that you need God. You cannot go it alone. Develop a relationship with God or improve the one you have. Seek God daily, not just when times are tough. He will see you through it, but you must put your faith in Him. Remember your loved one is with God (healed and happy) and you will see that person again. Most of all, when you feel alone, know that you are not because God is right beside you, loving

you. Finally, as quoted in Rob's Memorial Memory Card, "...bury your sorrows in

doing

good deeds."

Eulogy of Robert N. Tittenhofer, Jr.

Because of Rob's illness we were forced to consider our own mortality more often than most. Having had those talks, I can tell you that Rob always said, "When I am gone, baby, you have a big party, and don't let people be sad." How ironic it is that today is the very day I had planned a surprise party to celebrate Rob's life.

I only had Rob as my husband for five years, but we were friends nearly twenty. In that time, Rob gave to me a love that was so huge it will fulfill me for a lifetime. When I first learned that Rob had left this earth, I felt cheated beyond imagination. Today, looking around this room, I no longer feel cheated. I feel blessed to have had Rob even if the time was short. Rob made the world a better place, and Rob made me a better person.

For those that know me as well as Rob, you know I am rarely at a loss for words. Rob was the only one who could do that to me. The first time I met Rob some twenty years ago, he was so handsome that I could barely speak. Other times he left me speechless because he knew something about everything, and I simply had nothing intelligent to add. Today, I can barely speak again. Funny how Rob could make me this way.

So, I'm going to close with a few thoughts that I hope will comfort you as Rob asked me to do. I'll let others share their stories about times spent with Rob. I'm sure the stories will give Rob and all of us a good laugh.

Remember that Rob does not want sadness in our hearts, so find peace instead. Remember that Rob is healed now. Remember he left this earth doing something he loved so much. Remember that Rob loved and enjoyed every second of his life. Remember that he loved you all. Remember Rob's wit and humor. But most of all, remember to bury your sorrows in doing good deeds.

RESOURCES

Resources for *"For the Love of Cancer –*
A Passionate Pursuit to Understand Life, Death and Spirituality"

Hello From Heaven! – Bill and Judy Guggenheim

Into the Light – Dr. John Lerma, M.D

I'm Grieving as Fast as I Can – Linda Feinberg

Return from Tomorrow – George G. Ritchie with Elizabeth Sherrill

The Purpose Driven Life: What on Earth Am I Here For? – Rick Warren

It's Not About the Bike: My Journey Back to Life – Lance Armstrong

The Birth Called Death – Kathie Jordan

Love Your Life: Living Happy, Healthy and Whole – Victoria Osteen

Our Invisible Allies: The Definitive Guide on Angels – Ron Phillips

The Holy Bible

CPSIA information can be obtained
at www.ICGtesting.com
Printed in the USA
LVHW111639110522
718513LV00006B/129

9 781643 980386